IT'S MORE THAN YOUR FOOT

IT'S MORE THAN YOUR FOOT

Elite Kicking in Australian Football

Ben Moore

COPYRIGHT © 2017 BEN MOORE
All rights reserved.

IT'S MORE THAN YOUR FOOT
Elite Kicking in Australian Football

ISBN 978-1-61961-534-2   *Paperback*
      978-1-61961-535-9   *Ebook*

INTERIOR DESIGN BY
Kevin Barrett Kane

*To the players, coaches, medical &
conditioning team, and football department
of the Sydney Swans football club—thanks
for a lifetime of memories.*

ACKNOWLEDGMENTS

The Swans is a great community, full of good people. I was lucky to be at the club during a great period. To the following for helping me form the ideas which make up this book:

Stuey – thanks for the great pictures! Watching you teach and mentor players, coach on game day, and kick a ball, gave me an education in AFL football.

Spurrsy – thanks for the initial tour around the club and for introducing me to the coaches. That was a sliding-doors moment in my life.

Cahilly – you squeezed a pom into your already crowded office and taught me about the Swans. Conversations with you about skills, learning and football were always enlightening.

Horse – thanks for making me part of the team back at the beginning. I'll always remember the conversations we had about coaching and learning philosophies over the years.

JB & H – thanks for discussing the ideas in this book with me for (many) hours, and for making them better. I'm sure you wanted to say 'Stop it now' a few times when listening to me, but you never did.

Smithy – remember that holiday program? You've taken the Academy a long way since that. You and Cahilly compete for most laughs-per-minute across my time in Sydney.

George & DC – calming influences within the storm of an AFL season. I always felt better about the world after a conversation with you.

Roosy / Andrew / Deano / Tom – thanks for employing me at the beginning, and as time went on!

TABLE OF CONTENTS

INTRODUCTION / 1

PART ONE
The Method

1 Momentum / 21

2 Alignment / 35

3 Follow Through / 49

PART TWO
The Body

4 The Legs / 59

5 The Arms / 71

6 The Hands / 81

PART THREE
The Mind

7 Accepting Mistakes / 93

8 Feedback Mechanisms / 99

9 Goal Kicking / 109

10 Field Kicking / 127

CONCLUSION / 137

ABOUT THE AUTHOR / 141

INTRODUCTION

In many ways, the pursuit of athletic excellence is a matter of competing against and improving upon less skilled versions of oneself. Those hoping to participate in a given sport must first learn the skills necessary to play, and if they hope to compete in the sport's upper echelons, embark upon a perpetual effort to refine those skills into ever-increasing levels of proficiency.

Sometimes this process of self-improvement is performed largely at one's own direction. In other cases, a coach or an entire staff of coaches are employed to guide and shape the athlete's growth. And there are still other approaches that combine the two to bring about the levels of skill necessary to compete at a sport's highest level.

Regardless of the circumstances under which an athlete is trained, the learning process for complex movement skills can be improved drastically if it's based around a fundamental methodology that can be applied to any player—a framework that can be easily described to assist athletes of any type, operating at any level. In other words, it must be appropriate for players irrespective of their individual style of play, body shape or unique physiology.

One of the hallmarks of such a strategy is that its principles must incorporate the practices of the most accomplished players participating in the sport in question—i.e. the movements they actually undertake to hit the ball to various parts of the ground, or kick the ball in various situations. Any approach that lacks that essential quality contradicts what's been proven to work, likely leading to frustration on the part of the athletes attempting to implement the program. In fact, it may be actively preventing them from achieving success.

In the absence of a unified movement and learning methodology that describes what the top players are doing, it can be quite difficult for junior players to rise to a similar level. I first noticed this when playing and coaching cricket in England—the MCC coaching manual didn't and still doesn't describe what Bradman, Lara, Barry Richards, Gilchrist and others actually do with the cricket bat. Later, it was also apparent in the sport of Australian football when working as skill acquisition coach for the Sydney Swans football club.

It was the latter of these experiences that served as the inspiration for this book, and it all started in 2008 while I was studying for a master's degree in sport and exercise science at the University of Sydney. At the time, the Swans were the only professional football club in Sydney, competing in the country's premier sanctioning organisation: the Australian Football League.

As luck would have it, the team's coaching staff were interested in employing someone whose skillset included a knowledge of motor learning, cognitive psychology and the acquisition of physical skills—all topics I was studying as part of my master's degree program, and had studied previously when acquiring a bachelor's degree in the same field at the University of Birmingham. I combined the science I was learning with my own personal experiences in cricket to develop a few ideas on how they might be applied to the AFL. The Swans' head coach, Paul Roos, was a famously open-minded bloke who was willing to experiment with unconventional ideas garnered outside the sphere of the AFL, and ultimately agreed to bring me on under a short-term contract during that season.

Although it wasn't my first experience coaching—I had helped direct a number of amateur cricket teams in an addition to playing on them—it was my inaugural foray into the world of Australian Rules Football, and in addition to being the only Englishman on the staff, I was also the only coach who had never played the sport at its highest level.

In fact, I had never played it at all, which proved to be a double-edged sword. On one hand, it provided me with a unique perspective free of the biases and assumptions that are an inherent part of firsthand experience. Looking at the game from an outsider's point of view, I was free to question the conventional wisdom in ways that might not occur to someone who grew up with it, something that ultimately proved beneficial for my role.

But being an outsider wasn't always easy. It also meant I needed to learn the game, requiring me to spend my first several months observing and absorbing the thoughts and philosophies of the team's players and coaches. I knew my ability to provide meaningful input would hinge on understanding what players were trying to do, what they were trying to avoid and the history of what had been done before.

In an effort to accelerate my learning curve, I watched hours of videotaped practice sessions and kicking drills. As I progressed, I came to realise the team—and indeed the sport as a whole—seemed to lack a consistent methodology describing the process of learning to kick that also described the actions of the league's best players. It was the same problem I'd endured while playing cricket in the UK: just as no one could describe what the league's premier batsmen were doing during their innings or how they approached batting, there was no universally agreed-upon framework for how footballers should be conceptualizing the movement of kicking.

It wasn't long before I realised I needed to identify and explain a set of unifying principles for goal kicking that could be applied to any athlete, regardless of whether he was a 6'10' key position player or a 5'6' small forward.

My goal wasn't to create a specific style of kicking, the minutia of which would necessarily hinge on how individual athletes move their body and how the body in question is built. Instead, I felt that there must be some set of underlying principles that applied to every athlete, and so I set out to find them, eventually developing a plan with the rest of the coaching staff that could be put into place during the following preseason.

Although the Swans had been historically successful (they won the league premiership in 2005 and placed second the following year), 2009 represented a bit of a lull for the otherwise triumphant club, which registered just eight wins and failed to qualify for the finals for the first time since 2002. However, the players, coaching, recruitment and conditioning teams were building foundations that allowed us to turn things around over the course of the next several seasons, ultimately winning the premiership again in 2012 and finishing runner-up during the 2014 season.

One small part of these results was an improvement in goal kicking accuracy over an extended period. Looking at all games from 2003 to 2008, the Swans were ranked 11th for set shot conversions in what was then a 16-team league. But for all shots on goal during games in the period 2009 to 2015, we ranked second. We also jumped from last place to fifth in total accuracy on goal between 2008 and 2009, and were one of only two teams to finish in the top eight for set shot conversion in five of the seven seasons from 2009 to 2015.

As my time living in Sydney came to a close in 2015, it became clear to me that my observations differed from some established protocols for teaching and developing kicking skill and might assist coaches in instructing beginners or elevating the skills of more developed athletes. And while I would hesitate to say the method we developed in Sydney is the final word on the mechanics of kicking, it's certainly a proven approach that can result in observable improvements for kickers regardless of their existing skills or abilities.

It's also quite different than the instructional systems currently being used by most junior football clubs across the country. Rather than looking at a player's technique from a short term perspective and correcting specific aspects of their kick, this method calls for a holistic, long term approach geared toward improving an athlete's overall movement capacity. And make no mistake: adjusting a movement as complex as a kick takes a considerable amount of time, particularly when athletes are accustomed to performing the movement a certain way.

Just consider how long it takes a human being to learn to walk, hit a ball, or ride a bicycle—all skills which require incremental improvements made over a long period of time. It would be foolish to assume meaningful changes to a competitive athlete's kicking skill could be made with a 20-minute training session, no matter how inspired the responsible coach may be.

Particularly at the junior level, some coaches seem to believe 'correcting' singular aspects of an athlete's form qualifies as sufficient instruction (in fact, this applies to many sports, not just AFL). However, it should be clear by now that a more process-oriented approach is necessary to create significant change in a skill as complex as kicking a football.

After all, kicking a football is difficult. Bouncing an oval-shaped ball off the convex surface of one's foot into a goal that's seven meters wide—or toward a team-mate down the ground—is tough enough on its own. Add in the 35 other players involved in the game (and the fact that most kicks originate 40-50 meters away from their intended target) and it's not hard to see how lengthy and complex the learning process can potentially be.

Accordingly, the aim of this book is not to offer athletes a revolutionary new technique for kicking that will shock their opponents or awe competitors. That would imply that there exists a perfect approach to kicking. That simply isn't true, which is why advocating for or against specific techniques isn't my purpose at all. Instead, I hope to offer up a set of global principles that I observed while reviewing every single kick made by a

Swans player—and many made by opposing teams—during my seven years as skill acquisition coach. Once those underlying principles are understood, athletes and coaches should be able to apply them to improve kicking skills through every phase of the game.

That said, some of these concepts may seem counterintuitive to those who have grown up playing the sport. Football has been deeply ingrained in Australian culture for decades, and it's likely that the current generation of young people participating in the sport are playing for the same club or school that once featured their fathers and grandfathers. As with any sports boasting such rich tradition, it's not hard to imagine that a certain set of beliefs and behaviors might take hold, whether beneficial or otherwise.

Combined with the ongoing expansion of the sport nationwide, this ubiquity has given rise to a degree of dogma regarding what constitutes proper kicking technique as well as the means by which it's coached and learned. For example, a great deal of discussion centers around performing the kick as if the movement occurs along one or two planes: athletes must kick 'straight' in the sense that the ball should drop directly in line with the kicking leg, which itself must swing straight underneath the body, propelling the ball straight at its desired target.

While that philosophy has its merits, a careful inspection of the movements involved in a drop punt can also reveal some of its flaws. One need only consider the rotation at the pelvis and hip that must occur to lift the leg in order to understand a kick isn't simply a straight-line process—a point easily demonstrated by trying to maintain balance while putting one's weight on only one leg. Remaining upright in this position requires the non-weight-bearing leg (i.e., what would be the kicking leg) to shift slightly outward, meaning that, contrary to conventional wisdom, successful kickers aren't dropping the ball down in a straight line with the kicking leg. They're dropping it slightly outside so that it intersects with the arc of the kicking leg as it moves from behind the non-kicking one.

This behavior is observable in kicks executed by all the top players in the AFL. Whether required by a game scenario or due to personal preference, many of them kick with a pronounced arc that makes the path of their kicking leg look more like a 'J' or even a 'C'* than anything that could be described as 'straight'. As you might expect, this forces them to approach their target with a trajectory that angles slightly away from their kicking leg rather than dead-on straight—further evidence of the fact that successful kicking can occur even when the athlete isn't perfectly 'straight'. Figures 3 to 6 in Chapter 2 illustrate different levels of this kicking 'arc', ranging from a more 'straight' approach in Figure 3 to the more extravagant arcs in Figures 5 and 6.

The sport's conventional wisdom also includes a number of dictates regarding the ball drop. One example is the notion that kickers must make every effort to reduce the distance between their hand and their foot before releasing the ball. If

---

* These descriptors were originally used by Dave Alred, an English rugby coach.

such dogma proved true in a game environment, the AFL's top kickers would be seen leaning forward over the ball prior to executing their best kicks—essentially the opposite of what even casual fans of the sport observe on a regular basis.

Instead, successful kicks are routinely made by athletes standing straight up, and even leaning back to a certain degree, with the ball held high and their arms extended in front of them. Why? Because the extra space between their hand and their kicking leg allows them time to swing the kicking leg through powerfully and into the follow-through portion of the movement.

That combination of time and distance, colloquially referred to as the ball drop, is also the subject of a disproportionate amount of focus on the part of coaches and athletes alike. Although undoubtedly important, the sheer volume of scrutiny placed on each player's drop far outweighs the attention paid to other phases of the kick, amplifying its impact to such a degree that the other aspects pale in comparison.

One simple way of viewing a kick is to look at it as being composed of three distinct phases: its beginning, the point at which contact is made with the ball, and the follow-through movements that take place after impact to take the kick to its end point. Viewed from that perspective, individual elements of a kick, such as ball drop, are only a fraction of the total movement, whereas the beginning and ending portions occupy a much larger percentage of the action. With that in mind, it makes sense to shift focus during practice and learning onto foundational fundamentals like beginning and ending the movement in a physically stable position.

It's More Than Your Foot

In no other phase of the game is this focus more paramount than during a set-shot goal kick, a time when many athletes can be observed standing around, fiddling with the ball or moving from side to side before beginning their run-up. By eliminating these actions during practice in favor of a more stable beginning, and then ending the movement in a similarly stable condition, athletes are better positioned to gather feedback on what's taking place during the kick itself—and what they might want to improve.

The same principles can be applied after impact has been made with the ball. Too often, athletes will simply veer left or right and fade away after their foot makes contact, indicating a lack of awareness regarding what's happening with their body in the post-impact phase. Much like the ball-drop portion of the movement, players tend to overanalyze the specifics of how contact was made rather than taking a broader view that includes what happens before and after that point. But those phases are at least equally important, and performed in practice with appropriate focus, can provide valuable feedback regarding why the ball traveled along a specific path and how the kick felt to the athlete on an instinctual level.

By coming to a complete, deliberate stop when completing each kick in a practice environment, players can reinforce the notion that the movement process extends well beyond dropping the ball and connecting their kicking foot with it—concepts that are readily apparent in other sports. Consider the game of basketball, where players taking free throws regularly pause after the ball leaves their hand. The same phenomenon can be seen among place kickers in rugby, where perceptive viewers will notice a brief freeze in the moments following a kick. And perhaps most famously, golfers sometimes let their putts travel as far as 20 feet before taking a single step.

These activities aren't undertaken simply because athletes want to admire their work. They're done because, over time, participants in these sports have learned that taking a moment to reflect on what they've just done is a great way to acquire the feedback needed to improve their skills when they take their next shot or kick.

That said, athletes should not allow the binary outcome of a given kick to be the most important feedback they'll receive. On the contrary, it's of paramount importance that athletes make every effort to detach their emotions from the outcome of their kicks. Players will benefit from practice feedback to a much greater degree if they're assessing the action objectively rather than based on their subjective interpretation of whether the result was 'good' or 'bad'.

After all, a practice kick can be judged any number of ways. For example, a player could determine its value relative to its intended target, base his opinion on the crowd's reaction to his performance, or concern himself with the coach's opinion of his form. Worrying about these factors during practice can only distract a player from that which should be at the top of his mind: being connected to the physical process and gaining feedback that can be used to improve.

That can only be done if the athlete undertaking the kick is focused on controlling his body and the ball. Eliminating anxieties related to the binary outcome of the kick is one of the most important ways to achieve this level of focus. Once that's done, the physical process can take center stage, and it will remain so throughout the course of an athlete's career.

Compared to some of the coaching dogma that permeates the sport at the moment, these concepts may represent something of a departure from the norm. As coaching methodologies from a very junior level and upwards become more rigid nationwide, an increasing number of athletes are being pigeonholed into kicking with a 'standardised' technique based on many of the points discussed above.

This coaching situation is partially driven by the increased commercialisation of the game. The sale of television rights, in particular, has led to an influx of money for professional clubs at the highest level, resulting in larger coaching staffs and more generously compensated players who might have needed part-time jobs had they played just two decades before. Today's professional teams boast huge sport science and medical departments, conditioning coaches, player welfare managers, and assistant coaches for virtually every position on the field. And that's to say nothing of the high salaries claimed by some of the game's highest paid players.

In and of itself, this growth isn't necessarily a bad thing. In fact, I probably wouldn't have been offered a job in the first place had it not occurred. But, as with most developing and evolving institutions, not all of the changes resulting from this commercialisation are necessarily beneficial to the long term wellbeing of the sport itself or its players.

One of the side-effects is that it's given rise to a more formalised structure for teaching its fundamentals to children and preparing them for competition at amateur, metropolitan, state, and national levels. Academies are organised in an effort to 'fast-track' the skills of junior level athletes so that they'll be better suited for elite-level football sooner, and a great deal of effort is put into identifying talented young players so they can be scouted for the professional game.

To aid this process, organisers usually develop a standardised curriculum by which the athletes are judged. In and of itself, this isn't a bad thing, as having a documented standard provides coaches with targets and programs helpful in assisting younger players reach their full potential. But, as illustrated above, it has also resulted in the creation of certain structures for the performance and coaching of specific movement 'techniques' which may emphasise many of the wrong points or straightjacket an athlete's style.

Rather than being coached to adopt a specific 'technique', developing athletes should be encouraged to experiment with all methods of delivering the ball to a target location—even when the methods used differ from the standardised orthodoxy discussed above.

There is a clear difference between this more formalised style of learning and the way many of the league's top kickers, as well as most of my colleagues on the Swans' coaching staff, learned the fundamentals of the sport. Often, they discovered its principles organically by kicking a ball around a playground with older, more experienced children or after school with their parents. It goes without saying that these daily recreational activities played a fundamental role in developing their kicking skills during their formative years.

By contrast, today's generation rarely carries a ball to school at all. In fact, some schools have banned footballs entirely over the course of the past 10-15 years, helping to usher in an age of organised practice at the expense of self-directed free play. Thus a situation has arisen where fewer potential footballers learn the skills of the sport casually, and those who do experience it through the filter of a more formalised coaching framework.

This methodology has the potential to detract from some aspects of an athlete's development, and perhaps more importantly, it's wholly unnecessary. Part of what makes an activity like kicking so beautiful is its accessibility: kids can go out and learn to do it correctly without the assistance of an adult, simply by watching and imitating others. The human brain has a remarkable capacity for this type of learning that all but eliminates the need for a formal program, which is why sports like Australian Rules Football were able to produce elite competitors prior to becoming commercialised to the degree that they are today.

After all, top players weren't simply born with the abilities of an elite-level kicker. Genetics and natural talent probably played a role in their success, but even with those advantages, they still needed to practice in order to learn the fundamentals of the movement. And the stories one often hears regarding the nature of those practices almost always hinge on frequent sessions of spontaneous experimentation.

Free of verbal external feedback or the constraints of a training program, they fooled around with all sorts of methods for delivering the ball to a target—a healthy variety useful in learning how to undertake ball-related skills. Of course, most of those who developed their skills using these instinctual capacities likely couldn't verbalise or quantify precisely what actions or movements they take to correctly kick a ball. They might be able to hint at some elements of their approach, but for the most part, the physical action does not rely on an analytical part of the brain and can therefore be difficult to fully describe. Even if it weren't, it's likely that the learning process itself took place too long ago and at too young an age to be remembered with any degree of accuracy.

In other words, these top-level players (and former players turned coaches) are at a more advanced stage of learning where they are able to coordinate their movements with the surrounding environment—with very few thoughts that could be verbalised. By contrast, less developed skill levels usually involve players who are able to do something with concentration, but unable to perform the activity as consistently or as quickly, whilst it also requires more physical and mental effort (perhaps using a number of 'rules').

Or, as martial arts icon Bruce Lee said, 'Before I studied the art, a punch to me was just like a punch, a kick just like a kick. After I learned the art, a punch was no longer a punch, a kick no longer a kick. Now that I've understood the art, a punch is just like a punch, a kick just like a kick'. In other words, Lee moved from a position of complete misunderstanding to one of thought-process verbalisation before arriving at one of complete control.

One of Lee's points was that making an alteration to a skill will often require an athlete to willingly take a step backward on this ladder in order to intellectualise the desired adjustment. This is why it's not uncommon to see the performance of adult athletes suffer when making changes to their skillset—or to see wide variations in the performance of junior athletes learning a new sport. The movement in question tends to get worse before it gets better, ultimately resulting in the desired improvement only if the player can push through this often painful period.

It's something players will probably experience as they work to implement the methodologies discussed in this book. And from the athlete's perspective, there's often a tendency to view the effort as counterproductive due to the resulting frustration—something coaches can help alleviate by continually communicating that the players have generous amounts of time and space to improve their abilities. Certainly, a coach should expect his charges to enjoy the sport, do things well and continually improve, but he must also let them know he doesn't expect large-scale change to happen overnight.

With that kind of low-pressure mentality in place, it's more likely that junior level athletes will continue self-directed practice on their own and professional footballers will gain more knowledge from the practice environment. After all, enjoyment leads to motivation, which in turn leads to more practice. It's a cycle of self-improvement that can ultimately have dramatic results—and they'll take place in a far less painful manner, making the overall prospect of the effort more appealing to a broader range of athletes.

And rather than teaching them to conform their physical movements to some pre-existing standard or over-emphasising the minutia of the kicking action, coaches can provide players with a framework for the movement's essential components—leaving them free to develop their own style. By being made aware of these components and observing their effects on each kick, the athletes themselves will develop a greater understanding of what they're doing, both when the kick is successful and when it fails to reach its intended target.

Consider this book a roadmap describing how to get there, detailing a proven strategy for improving execution of the movement. By its conclusion, athletes and coaches alike will be better prepared to accept their mistakes, learn from the many sources of feedback the kicking movement can provide and facilitate self-learning for players at every level of the game.

First, we'll look at the foundational principles that can be applied to every type of kick made by every type of athlete: momentum, alignment and follow through. Viewed as a chain of events rather than individual points, these terms will serve as guides to each phase of the physical process, as well as a structure for learning, feedback and development

Once that's understood, we'll examine the mental aspects of both learning how to kick and improving one's existing skillset. Finally, we'll conclude with a look at specific components to the different types of kicks an athlete might encounter during the course of an AFL game or practice.

By the time we reach the conclusion of each section, players and coaches will be empowered with a practical means of teaching these philosophies while allowing for flexible technique.

PART ONE
THE METHOD

CHAPTER ONE
MOMENTUM

'When you first start to study a field, it seems like you have to memorise a zillion things. You don't. What you need is to identify the core principles—generally three to twelve of them—that govern the field. The million things you thought you had to memorise are simply various combinations of the core principles.'

– John Reed

It's a scene AFL fans see at one point or another in nearly every match they watch: having taken a great mark, a player is ideally positioned to make a seemingly straightforward kick with minimal distance between himself and his target. The kick itself is all but lined up for him—all he has to do is make it happen.

He stands at the end of his runup, carefully preparing for the kick both mentally and physically. Then, something unexpected happens. The kick skews or hooks off course, and the opportunity that moments ago seemed all but certain evaporates. It's not long before disappointed fans and commentators criticise the player for failing to practice adequately, or for choking under pressure.

Can you blame them? It's hardly unprecedented for an athlete to falter in a moment of pivotal importance, and it isn't difficult to see how the fast-paced nature of Australian Rules Football might increase the odds of this occurring. Conventional wisdom urges us to accept the simplest explanation as being the most likely, and chalking up a missed shot under such circumstances to mental failure certainly falls in line with that philosophy.

But is it really so simple? If fans and commentators could have witnessed the practices leading up to that missed kick, they would likely tell a much more complicated story—one from which footballers and coaches alike can draw valuable lessons.

In order to understand those lessons, everyone involved must first come to view the physical process of each kick as a chain of three phases: momentum, alignment and follow through. Each of these elements feeds into and affects the others, and are observable in any kick, regardless of the individual quirks or skill level of the athlete performing the movement. They don't describe a particular style, nor an ideal technique, but serve as identifiable terms that describe the progression of the action itself.

Kicking must be viewed as a whole body action, and these umbrella terms describe the gross physical process involved in this whole body action. Considered separate and apart from the minutia of the movement and even the outcome of an individual kick, they can serve as tools to facilitate learning, feedback and improvement during practice. The terms are:

- *Momentum* before, during and after the kick;
- *Alignment* at the point of impact and after impact; and completion of the kick with *follow through*.

To players and coaches performing at the highest levels of competition, these concepts may seem overly simplistic, but nearly every error committed in the game can be traced back to a mistake in one of these areas. And despite their obvious importance, it can take quite some time for players to understand and integrate them correctly during practice (and then in games).

Quantifying the individual phases into teachable terms allows even the most seasoned competitor to develop a greater understanding of actions they may currently be taking place instinctively. Over time, continual study, review and reinforcement of the elements' specific movements will allow players to self-correct in practice sessions. Later, they will be better prepared to incorporate more specific details addressed in this book regarding the actions of the hands, arms and legs.

MECHANICS

The first of these terms, *momentum*, is used in this context to describe the various actions a player might take to build up the force he will eventually exert on the ball. Regardless of any other factor in a player's kick, the ultimate goal is to apply this force to the ball in order to propel it forward, and in the AFL, that often means using a drop punt to send a ball over distances ranging between 15 and 65 meters. Kicks at the lengthier end of that spectrum require athletes to generate a substantial

Fig. 1

Example where the player builds momentum before the kick by running with the ball.

amount of force, and although such force is largely created by the muscular actions of the kicking leg, it's greatly assisted by movements that take place before the ball is dropped.

When this process is hindered in some way, it often leads to an outcome like the one from the example above. The causes are myriad: an athlete might have been struggling with set shot kicking over a long period of time, fatigued from a long game, or simply too concerned with not wasting a good opportunity. Whatever the cause, the end result is that he holds back on the physicality needed to generate good momentum—a mistake that could be avoided by practicing in a way that prepares him to 'switch on' at the start of a kick and deliver his foot to the ball with precision and power.

Of course, there's more to generating the momentum needed for a successful kick than simply running quickly prior to kicking, and it certainly isn't only a function of swinging the kicking leg with as much effort as a player can muster. There are also matters of timing to consider, whether created during the course of the run-up to the kick or by using the rotation of the hips prior to impact. And regardless of the type of kick being attempted, the player must ensure that this momentum is carried from the preparation phase or run-up that generates it into the actual impact with the ball and, beyond that, into the kick's follow-through.

One need only review the example in this chapter *(see fig. 1)* to see how different kinds of momentum generation might be required by different game or practice circumstances. Imagine two footballers, one who is running quickly at his target before attempting a kick, and another who is forced to begin the

Fig. 2

Example where the player generates momentum from a near-stationary position, by using greater pelvic rotation to 'kick across the body'. This method does not necessarily create more velocity on the ball, but it does allow a player to kick more quickly than the example in Kick 1 (e.g. when prevented from running forward by opposition players).

movement from a standing position with no run-up. Clearly, the two players in question will need to use different momentum generation techniques if they hope to successfully hit their target.

The running player doesn't need to swing his kicking leg in as wide and arc, or rotate his hips or pelvis as much as the one who's standing still. Why? Because the first player can simply transfer the momentum of his run into kicking the ball. The second player, meanwhile, will need a large rotation of his hips and pelvic region because he's generated less buildup in the moments before his foot makes contact with the ball. Consequently, he'll also need to drop the ball further outside his kicking leg to accommodate the way hip rotation alters the trajectory of the leg itself (producing a 'wider' swing of the kicking leg, as shown in Figure 2 in this chapter or Figure 4 in Chapter 2).

Such differences in momentum also alter other aspects of the kick's mechanics. Since the running player from the example above is effectively transferring his speed into the kicking action, the swing of his leg is generally going to appear 'straight up and down' (to use common AFL language). By contrast, the player coming from a near stop needs to generate power with only a few steps, requiring a dramatic rotation of the hips and pelvis that results in the application of a curved aesthetic to the kicking leg.

If the second player's kick goes wrong somehow, coaches and commentators will often assume the error is due to 'kicking across the body', implying that there must be some error in the player's technique. In reality, this is simply one of the many types of kicks a player will occasionally be forced to attempt.

The near-standstill used in this example may not be as common as other types of kicks, but situations do occasionally arise that call for such an effort, making it just as important to train that movement as ones originating from a flat-out run.

Neither is necessarily 'right' or 'wrong', but there is a clear difference between the two that can only be internalised with sufficient training in both—as well as the dozens of variations at different points along the continuum between those two extremes.

The vast majority of kicks will use some combination of these two types of momentum generation. When an athlete mixes the two in the wrong proportions, the kick often goes awry as it did in the example that opened this chapter. This typically manifests itself when athletes realise too late in the kicking cycle that they haven't built enough momentum and attempt to salvage a kick with the kind of dramatic hip rotation usually reserved for kicks with a shorter runup.

By attempting to generate the required force with a last-minute change in technique, athletes cause any number of problems. A common one is that the player will drop the ball too close to the center of their body or the line of the kicking leg, preventing the necessary hip rotation required to produce adequate force. They might also lose control of their non-kicking leg and side, causing the kicking leg itself to swing across the ideal line for best impact with the ball.

The result of either scenario is that the ball hooks to the left or slices to the right, the direction itself depending on whether the ball strikes the inside or outside of the player's foot. And because the events leading up to the failed kick are often subtle, it can be easy for coaches, spectators and even the players themselves to overlook the significant role momentum played in the end result.

Regardless of the specific type of method used to generate momentum, effective kicking relies on a player's ability to properly align parts of his body: the supporting foot is planted along a certain line, allowing the kicking leg to swing along a certain line prior to connecting with the ball. For kicks that occur on the run, most players will agree this requires smooth timing, good speed, control, even step length and a steady stride prior to the last step.

The final stride should be longer than the ones that precede it because this is how the stretch reflex is generated in the kicking leg. Rather than drawing the kicking leg back, players open out the final stride of the non-kicking leg, readying the kicking muscles for action in the leg that will ultimately apply force to the ball. It's during that final stride that the player's upper body will rotate and open in the direction opposite to the kicking leg hip in order to counterbalance the movement of the lower body. Generally speaking, the plant foot will typically land pointing toward the intended target line—although it might not in every case—and then the kick itself can commence.

Compare that to the results of attempting to generate last-second momentum with a dramatic rotation of the pelvis, which tends to push the kicking leg away from its intended path, resulting in a misaligned impact that ultimately causes an errant kick.

Of course, this isn't to suggest that rotation at the pelvis is necessarily a bad thing, only that the angles and setup of the kick must be properly adjusted to accommodate that type of momentum generation *(see fig. 2)*. For the player attempting a kick with a very short runup, rotation at the pelvis would be appropriate so long as the ball is dropped further outside the kicking leg, allowing it to swing through at a greater angle away from the body. In this scenario, the non-kicking sidearm should be drawn back further in order to prepare a stable position from which to kick.

It's not hard to see how awareness of these basic principles can improve kicking accuracy regardless of a player's specific style. In a set shot goal kick, for example, run-ups can vary wildly in terms of speed, length, and even the manner in which the player leans his body prior to impact, but everyone must carry momentum through the impact phase of the kick. Even players who 'lean back"—often derided by coaches who think this action detracts from the forward momentum of the kick—can be successful so long as they maintain stability in the stance of their non-kicking leg, hip, and upper body using their non-kicking-side arm.

TRAINING THE MOVEMENT

Awareness of these momentum principles should be used as a tool for providing feedback. By doing so, coaches can train players to set up momentum prior to executing their kicks, ultimately resulting in better accuracy as well as the ability to self-correct following failed attempts. In practice sessions, gaining this understanding can be aided with a simple activity using two lines of three cones placed 30-40 meters apart. Players at each of the two stations will then kick to each other off a varying number of steps using the following progression:

1. The player begins each movement on the rear cone, kicking the ball off of one or two steps.
2. Following impact with the ball, the player approaches the middle cone and receives a ball from a player performing the same drill at the opposite set of cones.
3. Using the second ball, the player then executes a kick on the run, using 5-6 steps to generate momentum before reaching the front cone.
4. The player returns to the rear cone and sets up to repeat the drill.

The purpose of the exercise is to focus purely on generating momentum while varying the number of steps participants may take before executing their kick. The initial kick should be performed with very little runup, while the second kick can be executed after four, five or even six steps based on the discretion of the coach running the drill.

Again, the ultimate goal isn't to perfect the players' kicking technique, but to acquaint them with the means of generating momentum in situations with varying amounts of space and time. Over time, internalising that knowledge will make it less likely for an athlete to misjudge the actions needed to generate proper momentum in a game environment.

DEPARTURE FROM CONVENTIONAL WISDOM

The concepts reinforced by the drill aren't new, and may even seem simple to players who can already kick well, but such fundamentals are rarely focused on or expounded upon to the degree needed for meaningful feedback or learning. And unlike the efforts to describe the performance of an ideal kicking style, the principles of momentum can be used as a flexible approach that could apply to any number of players, kicks or specific styles.

After all, the goal isn't to describe each of the individual movements that go into creating momentum, but instead to capture them under an umbrella term that can be used to encapsulate that portion of the kicking cycle. With the help of video feedback from a series of field or goal kicking sessions undertaken during a period of time, coaches can use that term and the concepts it represents to provide meaningful insights into players' kicking.

CONCLUSION

Regardless of an individual player's style, all athletes must generate momentum prior to making contact with the ball in order to apply the resulting force at impact. It's the first of three movement phases which occur in every kick, and executing it correctly is essential to the success of the overall movement. Here are three key points to remember when attempting to master the different kinds of momentum generation in practice:

- The momentum, alignment, follow-through model describes the gross physical process for every player's kick. It is also a structure for practice, feedback and learning.
- Momentum can be developed prior to ball contact by different combinations of running speed and pelvic/hip rotation. Momentum should be carried through a kick into the follow-through regardless of the method used.

- Movements in the upper and lower body (as well as relative angles in various parts of the body) will differ depending on the method used to generate momentum. Not adapting these movements when required to use a different method of momentum generation (e.g. kicking off one step) can often lead to errors with kicks.

By mastering those insights, players can reduce the odds of winding up in the unfortunate shoes of the athlete whose poor example started this chapter.

CHAPTER TWO
ALIGNMENT

'Learn the rules like a pro, so that you can break them like an artist.'
– Pablo Picasso

Imagine a junior level practice during which one of the youth players performs a kick with a pronounced arc in the movement of his kicking leg. He's a right footer who runs slightly toward the right of the target area rather than straight at it, then drops the ball outside the line of the kicking leg, which in turn swings through on an angle away from the center of the body as it makes its way toward impact.

Regardless of whether the ball travels directly at its intended target or veers errantly aside, it's likely to be met with the same reaction from the coaches in charge of the practice, who will probably criticise the player for 'kicking around corners' or not running straight at the target. They'll say he needs to 'straighten up his kicking', instructing the player to approach his target head on and kick the ball with a straight leg directly in line with the target.

Those same coaches might be surprised to learn that the kicking style they're attempting to alter looks quite similar to the one used by Stuart Dew, whose photo appears throughout this book. Dew is the senior assistant coach for the Swans, and was universally renowned for his kicking ability when he played for Port Adelaide and Hawthorn. In fact, Dew's kicking was widely praised by commentators and fans alike when Hawthorn won the 2008 premiership. A particularly inspired performance in the third quarter of the Grand Final resulted in no small measure of notoriety, and it was executed in the exact style so many coaches scoff at for violating the sport's orthodoxy of 'straightness'.

While that doesn't necessarily mean that every player needs to adopt Dew's kicking style to be successful, his ability to produce accurate, powerful kicks even when not 'kicking straight' does challenge the sport's conventional wisdom. So do the actions of many other AFL players, who regularly undertake successful kicks in the face of circumstances that preclude facing the target front-on.

MECHANICS

Of course, if an athlete has enough time to run straight at his target, then generally speaking, he will, and his shoulders and hips will face in that direction *(see fig. 3)*. In many ways, this makes a lot of sense, as a player will probably make fewer errors when executing kicks in this manner. But if this philosophy is the only one rehearsed in practice, it can cause significant problems.

After all, there are many game scenarios in which it simply isn't practical to run directly at the target. Even in situations where it can be done, there are a number of professional level players who choose not to, opting instead to angle slightly to the side of wherever they're aiming (to the right for a right-footer, or to the left for a left-footer).

Clearly, successful kicking can be done when the body isn't 'aligned' in a perfectly straight manner with the target. Yet despite this universally observable fact, some coaches continue to preach the straight-kicking Gospel. Doing so has the unfortunate side-effect of misleading players into believing the movement itself occurs only in straight lines along one or two planes. That simply isn't the case from a biomechanical perspective, and attempting to conform a kick to that orthodoxy can ultimately make it less accurate if this misconception is internalised.

Regardless of an athlete's unique style, the pelvis, hip joint, torso, and shoulders all must rotate in order to facilitate a powerful kick—even when they *are* running straight at the target *(see fig. 4)*. Attempting to suppress those essential movements in favor of lining up one's feet, pelvis, hip, waist, chest and shoulders with the target can cause issues with components of the kick. For example, the kicking leg will often 'swing across', with the ball impacting the inside or outside of the boot. This causes the kick to veer away from the goal or the teammate to whom a player is attempting to kick.

All of these problems can be avoided if players and coaches shift their focus to a broader view of overall alignment: one that emphasises awareness of the relative alignment of his feet, hips, chest and shoulders in relation to the ball and target. In other words, the kicker needs to be aware of the angles of his upper body, hips and legs in order to propel the ball in the correct direction and obtain feedback on the movement's execution.

Fig. 3

This example shows the kicker executing a set shot goal kick with the shoulders & pelvis (waist) lined up with the goal at the point of impact, and the kicking leg swinging through 'straight'.

This applies even if a player is 'kicking across the body' off of a one-step runup *(see fig. 5)*.

In fact, I would argue under-rotation of the pelvis, hips and shoulders is just as problematic in many situations as over-rotation. As we've already established, it's fundamental to the generation of power needed to perform a long-distance kick, but someone who has only ever practiced running straight at a target and kicking 'straight up and down' might be ill-suited to deal with the arc of the kicking leg that inevitably results.

When the distance of a kick is extended past a certain point, that lack of preparation can manifest itself in a number of ways. For example, the player sometimes constrains the movement unnaturally and is unable to generate enough power, or they try to force the kick at the last minute, probably dropping the ball too close to a line running down the center of their body. The kicking leg might then veer slightly to the outside of the ball in a futile attempt to compensate for the lack of power, causing the ball's trajectory to skew after it strikes the inside or outside of the boot.

Particularly in situations where an athlete is trying to generate substantial power with relatively few steps, these issues can be avoided by allowing for a more angled swing of the kicking leg, and therefore a greater rotation of the pelvis and upper body *(see fig. 6)*. In practice, players should be encouraged to take advantage of this strong rotation of the kicking side pelvis, hip, and leg as well as the anti-rotation of the non-kicking side—i.e., the non-kicking-side arm swinging forward as the trunk rotates opposite of the kicking side hip.

Mastery of these alignment principles helps the athlete create and maintain stability throughout the kick. The player aligns various parts of his body in the pre-kick phase and then maintains that alignment throughout the movement so that the non-kicking leg and hip can remain sturdy and strong. Since the non-kicking leg is what forms the foundation for a well-executed kick, it's imperative that it doesn't give way and collapse beneath the player.

The non-kicking arm drawing back and then closing in toward the kicking leg as it swings through toward impact assists the non-kicking leg in remaining strong (see frames 1 and 2 of Figure 4). The kicking leg pelvis and hip are then free to rotate strongly as the kicking foot moves toward impact and after it connects with the ball.

Although this biomechanical process occurs in every kick, its appearance and components are affected by the other factors of alignment—specifically, those of the footballer with his target. An athlete running directly at another player will have his plant foot, hips, and shoulders lined up with the target player as he executes the kick. But, as shown in figure 5, if the same athlete arcs out in a different direction, there will be a more obvious rotation at the hip, and the angle and trajectory of the kicking leg will be altered accordingly. The plant foot will still tend be placed so that it points generally toward the target, as will the hips at or just after impact. However, the shoulders will be more closed at impact when a player is kicking 'across the body' in this manner.

The nature of the game requires players to be flexible in their execution of kicks, and situations often occur which necessitate more rotation of the hips—and a greater angle of the kicking leg. Top-ranking players in the league understand that at an instinctual level and make no effort to restrict the rotation of their upper body and pelvis. Instead, they simply control them, harnessing both to fuel a powerful, accurate kick.

When these 'across the body' kicks are performed, the ball is dropped further outside the kicking leg than when running at the target, which allows the player to stand on the non-kicking leg and swing their foot through in a strong position. By contrast, if the ball were dropped directly in line with the kicking leg hip, it would prevent full rotation of the hips, ultimately reducing overall power. Since these kicks are required of and executed by professional players on a regular basis, they should be practiced by junior players beginning at a young age.

TRAINING THE MOVEMENT

There are a couple of activities coaches can use to assist players in their efforts to understand these concepts and harness them to their advantage. Arguably the simplest would begin by forming two lines of players standing shoulder-to-shoulder, with the lines themselves approximately 20 meters apart and facing one another.

Athletes in each line should be partnered with the player opposite them and kick the ball back and forth between them—while making conscious changes to the alignment of their bodies with each successive kick. Often, this will require deliberately turning away from a player's partner so that a kick must be made 'across the body'. The athletes should be encouraged to experiment, whether that manifests itself in the form of changing the direction their kicking foot points at impact or by trying different rotations of the hips and shoulders.

The ultimate goal of the activity is not to deliver the ball perfectly to its target on each kick, but to observe how different changes to the alignment of one's hips, feet, and shoulders affect how the ball must be dropped and the subsequent movement of the kicking leg required to hit the target. By focusing on these changes in trajectory, players will come to better understand how various postures are likely to change their kicks.

Another activity, perhaps best reserved for players practicing goal kicking specifically, involves creating a 'funnel' with two rows of cones pointed toward the goal. Coaches should then instruct the athletes not to necessarily run straight along the path of the cones, but to use them as a form of visual feedback, paying special attention to the way their bodies, the ball, and the goal align in relation to each set of guides.

Players should be encouraged to vary the angles at which

Fig. 4

This illustrates how the kicker uses strong rotation of the upper torso to counter the rotation of the pelvis. I call this 'anti-rotation' – i.e. the upper torso is rotating in the opposite direction to the pelvis. Here the pelvis (hips) and shoulders are lined up with the target at the point of impact.

Fig. 5

This example shows a kick 'across the body', where the player uses greater rotation of the pelvis in order to generate force into the kick.

they approach the target as well as the number of steps they take in the momentum phase of each kick. Some kicks will occur while running at the goal straight-on, while others will take place after a single step, requiring heavy cross-body movement. Many other attempts will occur at various points along the spectrum between those two extremes.

As we've already established, the components of those kicks will change at a biomechanical level in both drills, providing the players with an opportunity to internalise the importance of alignment. Executed correctly, they'll come away with a better understanding of how the alignment and angles of various body parts relative to the target affect how a kick must be executed in order to be successful. In other words, they'll come to understand how the angle of the non-kicking foot during the final stride affects how the ball must be dropped relative to the kicking leg—and therefore the path of the kicking leg—and,

It's More Than Your Foot

Fig. 6

Another example illustrating that a kicker does not need to line everything up straight in order to execute a successful kick.

finally, the trajectory along which the hips travel. This, in turn, affects the positioning of the shoulders and the angle of the chest according to the principles of rotation and anti-rotation.

DEPARTURE FROM CONVENTIONAL WISDOM

These concepts may seem like a significant departure from the norm, particularly for coaches and players participating at the junior level, where a great deal of time is spent learning what are generally considered 'the basics'. Unfortunately, the basics in question tend to overemphasise relatively simple points like 'straightening up kicking' at the expense of teaching more complicated movements.

Since the game environment often forces players to kick when they aren't running directly at their target, it's both appropriate and necessary for young athletes to learn how to undertake more challenging kicks—even in the early phases of their development. It's my view that instruction in these areas is every bit as much a part of learning 'the basics' as telling athletes to 'line up' with their targets.

Although running directly at the target is probably preferable for many players, it isn't ideal for every athlete or even possible in many competitive scenarios. The fact is, with enough practice, an athlete can kick at virtually any angle in front of them, assuming the target is to the inside of their kicking foot. That remains true whether they're facing their target straight-on or not.

Today's conventional wisdom suggests the opposite, and often gives athletes the wrong cues about what's important, insisting that running at the target should be a player's primary concern. In reality, an awareness of how much rotation is being used and the angle at which the ball is dropped relative to the kicking leg will have a much greater effect on the result of the kick.

Certainly, 'run straight at the target' is advice that can be of some benefit from a coaching and learning perspective, but at a certain point it will become a hindrance that limits a player's potential. Instead, footballers should be given the chance to understand they can kick many angles so long as they have an awareness of their foot, hip, and chest positioning as well as what's happening with their arms.

Experimenting with different alignments of various body parts will likely get a junior player derided as 'trying millionaire stuff', as opposed to the supposedly preferable blue collar approach of kicking within a narrow band of movement. Certainly, a coach doesn't want an athlete taking unnecessary risks in a game and turning over possession to the opposing team, but there should still be a time and a place for such work in the practice environment. At the more junior levels, I would argue it's absolutely essential.

It goes without saying that some of these more unorthodox kicks will not be successful in terms of reaching their target, but by using the methodology described in this chapter, coaches and players alike should be able to improve them the next time they're attempted.

CONCLUSION

The relative alignment of body parts before, during, and after impact is a crucial component of kicking accuracy that is rarely addressed to the degree its importance warrants. Conventional wisdom, particularly as it applies to athletes in junior leagues, remains too dependent on an oversimplified doctrine that fails to account for the myriad factors that may affect an athlete's performance in this phase of a kick. Instead, players practicing the principles outlined in this chapter should remember:

- 'Alignment' does not mean simply 'running straight at the target' or 'lining everything up with the target'.
- Players should practice being aware of the *relative* alignment of different body segments required to propel the ball successfully in various directions.
- This awareness, combined with maintaining dynamic stability throughout the kick (using 'anti-rotation' from the non-kicking side) is more important than trying to 'line everything up with the target'.

Practicing with these principles in mind has the potential to assist athletes at any level in improving the quality of their kicks. And who knows? With enough improvement, they may learn to kick like Stuart Dew.

CHAPTER THREE
FOLLOW THROUGH

'People say my kicking skills must be genetic, that I was born with these disposal skills. Well, let me explode the myth, because it was all due to hard work and practice. Get the basics right and practice them again and again and again.'

– Darren Jarman

Coaches and commentators often try to determine what aspects of a game have drawn a player's focus by looking at his eyes. Cricketers are routinely told to keep their eye on the ball, those who train competitive snowboarders and skiers often caution that where they look will determine their direction, and many other sports are marked by references to the placement of one's gaze.

With that in mind, observers of an AFL practice session will not be surprised to see athletes looking at the targets of their kicks, whether they be field kicks aimed at fellow players, goal kicks in general play, or set shots. While they obviously need to look at their target in order to plan the trajectory of an effort in the pre-kick period, players sometimes pursue this planning too zealously and end up eyeing their target before the ball has even hit the boot. Doing so may cause issues with a given player's power or accuracy, but perhaps more importantly, it often reduces the value of practice time.

This dynamic creates a vicious cycle: with each successive kick, the athlete's head comes up and back ever so slightly, the player himself more concerned with its outcome than with finishing the movement mentally or physically. Regardless of how the ball impacts the boot or the accuracy of the kick, this focus on outcome before the physical process has reached its conclusion creates a disconnect between the athlete's mind and his movements. It may also create physical issues that limit the amount of force he's able to exert on the ball.

Whether the kick is successful or not, the underlying problem remains that the athlete in question is failing to follow-through consciously with the mechanics of the kick, resulting in an incomplete movement that can negatively impact both its outcome and—more importantly—the value of practicing the move. Not only can the kick itself suffer, but the athlete is robbed of important feedback that is critical to the learning process.

Such feedback can only be gained when a player briefly holds the end position of the physical action, providing a moment of reflection similar to that used by a basketball player following a free throw. By contrast, footballers can often be seen running off line or falling away after impact, regarding follow through as an unimportant abstraction—if they think about it at all.

Fig. 7

Example of a kick where the player 'bounces' on his non-kicking (right) leg in the follow-through. This example is a set shot, and you are also likely to see this in field kicks executed off a limited number of steps.

MECHANICS

In reality, follow-through is a crucial element of each kick performed within the structure of a practice, and forms the foundation of skill development in addition to simplifying the conceptualisation of the kick itself. To realise those benefits, athletes and coaches alike must reframe the mental aspects of a kick as aiming for its conclusion—and stress the need for physical management until the kicker reaches an end position as opposed to believing the action ends when impact occurs with the ball (or before!).

This can be done a number of ways in practice, but it generally means allowing the kicking leg to continue along the ball's target flight path as long as possible before the athlete comes to a stop in a physically stable position which he then holds for a moment before moving on. The physical elements of the follow-through will vary according to the type of kick. While practicing a set shot goal kick, for example, the player will tend to bounce on his non-kicking leg after impact, then follow-through forward *(see fig. 7)*. This is also the case for a kick executed off one or two steps. By contrast, a kicker who's already on the move when he executes a kick will land on the kicking leg after impact and won't bounce on the non-kicking leg *(see fig. 8)*.

To emphasise again, follow-through is more than just a physical action. As we've already established, it's also a mental exercise that provides a brief moment to reflect on the action that's just been performed, accept feedback, and then use it to improve accuracy over time (even if most of this is done unconsciously). The mental component is so significant that it rarely happens naturally or magically—it must be trained and emphasised in a disciplined way.

TRAINING THE MOVEMENT

Coaches can facilitate a fundamental understanding of the concept and its importance using a series of short warm-up exercises: two based around player-to-player kicking, and a third involving goal kicking. For the first, players should line up about 15-20 meters apart and focus on landing deliberately on their kicking leg after making contact with the ball before doing a slow jog through the movement. The second drill can be performed from the same position, but rather than landing on their kicking leg, players should kick and then hop on the balancing leg once or twice.

Participating in these drills back to back helps players get a feeling for the two extremes of follow-through—hopping on the non-kicking leg during kicks with little room for building momentum, and stretching out and landing on the kicking leg during kicks with more forward motion.

An additional activity that assists in developing this understanding focuses solely on goal kicking. For this exercise, athletes can perform any standard goal-kicking drill, but should be required to do so with one added requirement: to count to three before looking up at the result of each kick. This brief delay further reinforces the need to focus on the movement itself rather than its outcome—something which, as mentioned above, tends not to happen in situations where knowledge of a kick's success or failure is readily available.

DEPARTURE FROM CONVENTIONAL WISDOM

In many ways, this understanding of follow-through may run contrary to some of the more prevalent views regarding its

It's More Than Your Foot

Fig. 8

Example of a kick where the player lands on his kicking (left) leg in the follow-through. This will likely be the case for kicks executed on the run.

value. In fact, some would say that any factor capable of affecting a kick's outcome has already come to pass by the time a player's foot connects with the ball. They also claim that follow-through has no bearing on the mechanics of the kick itself because the ball has already begun traveling away from the foot when this phase begins.

Another view of follow-through is that it's simply a physical process for slowing the kicking leg after impact. This view isn't necessarily incorrect—the slowing of the kicking leg will occur without conscious effort—but it fails to address the other benefits of proper focus on follow-through.

Such views fail to account for the fact that maintaining an awareness of the follow-through phase necessarily means putting into place the preceding elements of the kick needed to correctly achieve it (i.e., it is a feed-forward mechanism). As mentioned above, properly executed follow-through can only be achieved if the other phases of the kick are performed correctly—a fundamental truth that, by its very nature, ensures proper execution. And despite its position at the end of the Momentum-Alignment-Follow through model, it can and should be emphasised from the very beginning of practice.

None of this is to suggest players should be consciously concerned about follow-through in a game environment, where the presence of opposition players and the general chaos of competition necessarily limit opportunities for reflection. Instead, they should focus on it in practice sessions as a discipline in and of itself as well as a learning tool. They can then operate with a subconscious awareness of it in the competitive environment.

Thinking about creating a strong follow-through in practice

facilitates a feed-forward mentality that makes it likely for a kicker to successfully carry out earlier movements in the kicking cycle, using momentum and alignment to create a physically correct conclusion.

CONCLUSION

It's important to remember that follow-through is not a 'technique', as such. It's a learning and feedback tool, and a physical practice discipline. Accordingly, athletes and coaches should remember that:

- Every kick must be finished both physically and mentally.
- Follow-through is something an athlete can control regardless of outcome.
- It's a feed-forward physical process as well as one that generates feedback for learning.
- The physical mechanics of follow-through will depend on the circumstances of the kick.
- Although it's last in the Momentum-Alignment-Follow through model, practice *could* be conducted focusing solely on follow-through. This is because executing it properly will force players to complete the physical portion of the kick correctly.

By adhering to these principles, players and coaches alike will be able to create a more complete learning environment in practice which should translate to better performance on the field.

PART TWO
THE BODY

CHAPTER FOUR
THE LEGS

'*The exact contrary of what is generally believed is often the truth.*'
– Jean de la Bruyere

When a kick falls short of reaching its intended target, it's obvious to anyone watching that the athlete either made an error in the ball's placement on his boot or misjudged the force needed to propel the ball where he'd hoped to. What can be less obvious is why this took place, and more importantly, what might have been done to improve it.

Although there are a number of possible explanations, a coach or trainer observing this outcome might well begin diagnosing the problem by taking a look at the positioning and stability of the player's non-kicking leg. What they could find is that the supporting knee has bent excessively during the kick, practically collapsing under the athlete. The non-kicking side hip my also appear to have 'collapsed', and the action of the non-kicking side arm could appear weak. This destabilises the platform on which the movement is built, and diminishes its power.

A result of this instability may be an excessive twisting in the non-kicking side hip, causing the kicking leg to swing across the anticipated path of the kick. As a result, the ball strikes the boot in a slightly different position than expected and the kick suffers a decrease in accuracy in addition to the aforementioned loss of power.

MECHANICS

If this sounds familiar, it's because it also happened to the athlete from Chapter One who failed to build up enough momentum prior to the kick. Both problems result in overcompensation, causing a twist of the torso at the last second. These issues highlight the need to understand the kick as a sequence of events, rather than a simple strike of the boot against a ball. From there, it becomes clear that what initially appears to be an error at the end of the movement may actually be caused by something much earlier in the kinetic chain.

What at first glance looks like an error in a player's ball drop, for example, may actually be the result of the athlete's failure to extend his arms fully out in front of him before removing the non-kicking-side arm from the ball during the penultimate stride. Athletes and coaches are better prepared to provide or derive meaningful feedback from each kick if they have an understanding of the manner in which each successive phase of the movement affects the next.

One of the keys to developing that understanding is to examine the movements of each body part during the execution of a kick—ones that, much like the phases of kicking we've already discussed, are observable irrespective of the specific style with which the movement is performed *(see fig. 9)*. With respect to an athlete's legs, that means focusing on the crucial moments which occur in the final two strides taken prior to connecting with the ball. It's during these two steps that the timing of the kick will be determined.

As the kicking leg swings forward in the penultimate stride, the ball is moved up and forward with both hands. The specific height of the lift is dependent on the anticipated power of the kick; it's not uncommon to see it held nearly as high as the player's chest in the run-up to one requiring a large amount of force (as seen in frames 4 and 5 of fig. 9).

When the kicking foot nears the ground, the athlete's non-kicking hand leaves the ball in preparation for the final stride (as seen in frames 5 and 6 of fig. 9). The non-kicking leg then moves forward and the kicking leg stretches backward behind the body. It's this stretch that will generate the foot speed needed to complete the kick.

There are multiple factors that contribute to this buildup of energy, and they occur as a result of the upper body moving in concert with the lower body (as seen in frames 7 and 8 of fig. 9). The non-kicking arm should move up and backward with the hand above the shoulder, the lower back should extend, and as we've previously discussed, the pelvis will rotate on the kicking side and extend the hip.

Each of these movements is taking place as the non-kicking foot comes down and ball release occurs just before it makes contact with the ground (as seen in frame 8 of fig. 9). In this final stage, the non-kicking leg must flex to absorb the impact of landing, then brace and extend to create a base from which the kicking leg can swing through to connect with the ball (as seen in frame 9 of fig. 9).

Fig. 9

Fig. 9 cont.

The phases of a kick.

The positioning of the support foot at this point illustrates the importance of alignment, and will have a critical impact on the overall outcome of the kick. Frames 5-8 of figure 9 demonstrate the player setting up the relative alignment of the ball, non-kicking foot and kicking foot in order to execute the movement. If a player misjudges the placement of his non-kicking foot, either too wide or narrow relative to the ball, it may restrict the range of the kick or significantly reduce accuracy. After all, the path along which the kicking leg swings is a function of the movements that came before it. To clarify, it's not so much that the non-kicking foot needs to be 'aligned with the target', but more that the player must have positioned it correctly relative to where he plans to release the ball. If he misjudges placement, the athlete can often push the kicking leg out of line, increasing the likelihood of an errant kick.

Errors of this type may manifest themselves in the form of an exaggerated overstep: the player unintentionally crosses the body with the plant foot and fails to compensate by dropping the ball further outside the kicking leg. To avoid that scenario, players should focus on alignment, balance, and strength during the final stride—and pay attention to the alignment of the feet, hips, shoulders, and arms relative to the ball.

The player is then positioned for the next phase of the sequence: the forward swing of the kicking leg, which will ultimately generate the foot speed needed to propel the ball after impact (Frames 10 to 12 of figure 9). This movement should begin in the pelvis and hip, while the kicking-leg knee remains relatively flexed in order to maximise timing of its release. However, it's important that the player avoid over-bending the kicking leg knee behind him, as such movements necessarily restrict the essential extension of the hip.

As illustrated by the series of photographs in figure 9, the body moves like a whip: movement begins in the player's upper body and trunk, and is then carried through the pelvis, thigh, lower leg, and ultimately, the foot. It's a sequence of events that remains the same for every kick, with the specific range of motion determined by the length of the kick being attempted. The sequence leads directly into the next phase—impact with the ball.

Players generally aim to connect with the ball positioned as close to vertical as possible. Impact will occur slightly below the ball's center with a foot that's stiff at the ankle, forming a solid platform that effectively transfers its speed to the ball. While this is taking place, momentum generated in the pre-impact period will tend to mean that the player continues to move forward while his head and center of gravity shift from their position just behind the non-kicking leg to directly over it. Figures 7 and 8 from the previous chapter illustrate this phenomenon.

It's vital for players to maintain control of the rotational elements occurring during the action, regardless of whether they're kicking with a more orthodox, 'straight' style, or 'around the corner' like a rugby player. In both instances, there will always be rotation at the hip and pelvic region to maintain balance on the support leg while generating force with the kicking leg. The upper torso also rotates, aided by the non-kicking-side arm, in order to counter the force and rotation of the kicking hip. Knowing that these actions will occur, it's important for players to be aware of, plan for, and exert control over them so that they can be harnessed successfully.

As the kicking leg swings forward, athletes must also be aware of the its tendency to slide across in the direction of the support leg—a common error with the potential to throw a kick out of alignment. Maintaining a feeling of strength through the non-kicking side, from the knee to the shoulder, will allow players to successfully complete the leg swing as planned. Aiming to keep the kicking foot moving toward its target in the split second after impact is also useful in practice. The follow-through movements described in Chapter Three then conclude the motion.

There is a clear rhythm to the series of events, and they occur in every kick, whether executed with a lengthy run-up or after a single step. Even when a player kicks from a stationary position off one step, one will notice a slight, initial backward movement with the non-kicking leg in order to create the same timing sequence.

Being aware of the sequence allows players to obtain feedback on each of the individual factors involved rather than focusing purely on the ball hitting the foot. That awareness can ultimately be used to improve power and accuracy—if practiced over a period of time.

Such practices should also include elements which teach the player to pay close attention to their footwork, as executing it improperly can easily interfere with the mechanics of a kick. There can be a temptation for athletes to over-stride in the run-up to a kick in an effort to produce more power. During the final stride, which should generally be slightly longer than the others, it's important to avoid over-exaggerating the movement.

Think of it instead as a slight lengthening designed to create hip extension, a distinction that can be facilitated naturally by viewing it as a steadying stride.

There are also situational factors to consider: if a player is required to turn toward the target on the same side as his kicking leg (i.e., to the right for a right footer), realigning his body can be a challenge. This is because the support foot must step across the kicking leg in order to open the body up toward the target, a movement often performed inadequately to the detriment of the kick's alignment and follow-through.

A weakness in the turn of the non-kicking leg not only spreads to the hips, it results in a failure to rotate the upper body away from the kicking leg. Those weaknesses feed forward into the non-kicking arm and hip, and the kick may be ineffective due to the collapse of the non-kicking leg.

TRAINING THE MOVEMENT

Given the relative complexity of all that goes on with the legs during a kick, it's not hard to imagine there might be any number of activities players and coaches can use to train them. That said, the following three routines may prove useful when undertaking practice based on the principles outlined in this chapter.

The first of these is designed to build adaptability to changing circumstances, and should be performed with a soccer ball. Players should be asked to line up facing a wall or other immovable surface and kick the ball into it repeatedly, adjusting as needed each time the ball rebounds toward them. Coaches can instruct the players to reposition themselves at any number of distances, necessitating different timing and force requirements that will force the players to adjust the movement accordingly. Ultimately, players should aim to reposition the non-kicking foot with each iteration so that the kicks can be executed in rapid sequence.

Another activity that may help train awareness of the leg movements involves forcing players to operate at extreme ends of the stride spectrum: athletes should execute a number of kicks on the run using excessively long strides, followed by a number of kicks using extremely short ones. In doing so, they should seek feedback on how the different stride lengths affect the kick itself, and what actions must be taken in other parts of the body to compensate.

Finally, athletes could repeat the training activity from Chapter One, but shift their focus from momentum generation to the various step lengths and leg angles required to propel the ball across different distances.

DEPARTURE FROM CONVENTIONAL WISDOM

Although the techniques and principles outlined in this chapter don't depart from conventional wisdom, the importance of the non-kicking leg—and how both legs work in concert with the upper body to create timing in a kick—can be under emphasised. Both legs obviously play a crucial role in 'alignment' for a kick, but that role is more complex than simply swinging the kicking leg at an intended target. Hopefully, it should be clear that they're too important to be disregarded in this manner, and correcting that imbalance can be done by applying the concepts discussed in this chapter.

CONCLUSION

Taking a closer look at the movement of the legs—or any of the other limbs mentioned in this section—should not be viewed as a substitute for training under the Momentum-Alignment-Follow through model. Instead, taking these observations into account should be viewed as ancillary information to assist in applying the training model outlined in chapters 1-3. With that in mind, here are three key takeaways regarding the movement of the legs:

- The non-kicking leg is just as important as the kicking leg in producing powerful, accurate kicks.
- Both legs work together with the upper body during the final two strides to create timing in a kick.
- A kick's alignment is set up in the pre-impact phases using both legs and the upper body.

As we continue to move forward with this discussion of the limbs, players and coaches should keep the training model from early chapters in mind and apply any new knowledge gained from this section to its practice.

CHAPTER FIVE
THE ARMS

'If you only read the books that everyone else is reading, you can only think what everyone else is thinking.'

– Haruki Murakami

From the day an Australian Rules Football player first learns of the sport and until he plays his last game, he will hear an incalculable number of references to the importance of proper 'ball drop'. To a certain degree, that emphasis makes sense: clearly there is an inherent difficulty in dropping an oval ball in such a way that it points upwards at the exact moment one's foot swings through it, which is what a footballer is aiming to do.

Particularly for athletes in the early stages of learning the sport, coaches often look to mitigate these difficulties by simplifying and restricting the movement. At the most basic level, they might encourage athletes to stand completely still with their arms hanging down with the ball aligned over the kicking leg, so that it only drops a foot or so before connecting with the boot. Players may also be told to hunch over a bit, holding the ball as low as possible in order to maximise the likelihood that the ball drop will be an 'accurate' one. There are countless other practices designed to minimise the possibility of error in this phase of the movement, all of them restrictive to one degree or another.

The problem with these methods is each of them tends to reduce or inhibit the correct movement of the arms in front of the body during the pre-kicking phase, which is absolutely critical to the timing of a kick, and therefore its accuracy and power. Players often appear 'crunched up', or hunched over, which restricts movement in the upper body and the hips—and their performance suffers as a result.

Another common error produced by this approach is the tendency for kickers to hold onto the ball with their non-kicking-side arm for too long, preventing the full extension and recoil needed to provide stability to the corresponding leg. After all, if the focus is solely on minimising air time between ball release and contact with the foot, it's only natural for the athlete to think he can't fully extend his arm or pull the non-kicking-side arm off early, which in turn disrupts the timing of the kick itself.

There's also a risk that players will interpret these movement-restricting instructions to mean they should also suppress the natural side-to-side sway of their shoulders while running with both hands on the ball. Attempting to restrict it negatively affects the accuracy and timing of the kick by weakening the movement of the non-kicking arm. Not only will it likely fail to fully extend, but the recoil needed to create extension across the chest will also be limited, tightening the shoulders and hampering the forward whip of the kicking leg.

Ironically, when a coach sees the unsuccessful result of any of these errors, it's often attributed to a failure to minimise air time between ball release and impact (i.e., ball drop).

Fig. 10

Fig. 10 cont.

Movement and coordination of the arms in preparing and executing a kick on the run.

MECHANICS

A review of any successful kick can provide clues as to why these errors cause an athlete's performance to suffer. In nearly every instance, the best kickers have both hands well out in front of their body before one comes off, leaving the kicking-side-arm directly in front of them at anything up to chest level (*see fig. 10 and 11*). The kicking hand cradles the ball rather than gripping it tightly, then comes down again just as the kicking leg swings up, ultimately resulting in impact.

This method produces successful kicks because it creates the additional space needed for the other movements in the action to take place: specifically, the positioning of the non-kicking leg, the swing of the non-kicking arm, and the swing of the kicking leg,

Of course, conventional wisdom suggests that this extra space only serves to increase the possibility of error, and to a certain degree that's true. Obviously, athletes want to avoid air time that doesn't meaningfully improve the quality of the kick. However, as demonstrated here, holding it to an absolute minimum is equally damaging to the likelihood of success.

Instead, players need to seek a middle ground between the two extremes, and do so with the understanding that the appearance of the kick will vary based on the distance being attempted. There may well be a decent swing of the arms on a short kick, for example, but the arms will rarely ever travel as high as the player's chest. In fact, bringing the ball to waist level is often all it takes to propel the ball accurately over 15-30 meters.

By contrast, longer kicks of 45 meters or more will require players to lift the ball higher, reaching chest level before the non-kicking-side hand is removed from the ball and the kicking hand moves down slightly before release (as in figure 10). In both cases, the movements themselves are the same—they're simply compacted for the shorter kick, occurring along an abbreviated timeline.

That said, the importance of properly placing one's arms extends well beyond simply creating a successful 'ball drop'. As we've already discussed, kicking is both an upper and lower body activity, but since most of the action takes place below the waist, the important upper-body portion of the movement is often neglected. The unfortunate side-effect of this mentality is that some critically important portions of the movement are undervalued.

Chief among these essential functions are what I've come to call rotation and anti-rotation: as one part of the body moves forward to facilitate the power of a kick, the opposite side naturally counters in the opposite direction to maintain stability and balance.

Imagine a left-footed athlete performing a set-shot goal kick. As his left leg moves forward during the kick, his right arm moves from a position slightly behind his body, rapidly traveling forward as the kicking leg approaches impact (see figure 3 in chapter 2). When his boot connects with the ball, the right arm is under his shoulder, and it continues on a forward trajectory as the ball departs for the goal. In other words, the left side of his body rotates to produce force needed to propel the ball, while his right side provides a balancing anti-rotational force that allows the ball to travel along a straight line.

The equal and opposite dynamic between the two movements

is what allows the player to remain upright and facilitates the timing of the kick, ultimately contributing greatly to its accuracy. After all, the kicking-side-arm must be extended out as the non-kicking leg plants in order to position the ball for release so that it can impact the foot accurately. In the absence of either of these actions, the athlete would twist wildly at the hips and shoulders due to the inertia of his kicking leg—and likely find himself unable to produce an accurate or powerful result.

TRAINING THE MOVEMENT

Strategies for internalising these concepts might take the form of several different activities depending on the level at which the athlete being trained is playing. At junior levels, it's imperative that coaches and players avoid drills that restrict the movement at the front of the kick so that the other movements are allowed to happen naturally. Opposite-side arm movement, in particular, can be greatly limited if the athlete doesn't extend the ball well out in front of his body.

Of course, training such broad movements at the junior level is complicated by the generally small nature of the athletes' developing hands, which may struggle to cradle an official Australian Rules football correctly. One way to adjust for that difficulty while still training the fundamentals of the movement is to use a smaller ball, perhaps even one with a round shape. Any number of different balls can be used, ranging from those meant for soccer to something the size of a tennis ball. Objects of different weights, sizes and shapes will obviously produce different results, but all will help players learn more about themselves and the physics relevant to their sport.

By freeing these young athletes from the need to focus on an AFL ball's unique shape and rotation, coaches can offer them additional time to focus on the movement holistically. This strategy can even be applied at more senior levels of the game if a particular player struggles with extending the ball sufficiently out in front of him. In both cases, it will promote a continued focus on creating space and openness in front of the body and condition athletes to avoid the hunched-over appearance that so often limits a kicker's performance.

More experienced players can gain additional benefits from these drills by paying close attention to the way a different ball forces them to vary components of their kicking movement in order to produce a desired outcome. Regardless, they should never forget that the primary purpose of exercising in this manner is to encourage players at all levels to get the ball well out in front of them prior to ball release. That's something that's just as necessary at the elite level as it is for beginning players.

Although double-handed ball-drops—ones in which the non-kicking-side arm doesn't come off the ball quickly enough—are more common in junior leagues, even the occasional AFL player is accused of the practice from time to time. In every case, it's almost always caused by problems with the timing and length of this extension at the front of the body. Arguably the most observable evidence that this is taking place is that the ball will drop too far toward the middle of the body as opposed to in line with or slightly outside of the kicking leg. This is a sign that the footballer is failing to extend his arms out far enough, and likely leaving the non-kicking-side arm on the ball too long, as well.

DEPARTURE FROM CONVENTIONAL WISDOM

I'm convinced that these training methods and the concepts they're based on will improve kicking ability for athletes at every level, but as with so many others discussed in this book, they probably don't receive the same level of attention as other aspects of the kick. The importance of openness and placement of the kicking-side arm is typically diminished compared to the overwhelming level of focus placed on minimising the ball's air time during the drop. As we've already discussed, clinging too tightly to this orthodoxy can actually act against proper functioning of the arms during a kick.

To see this difference illustrated in practical terms, athletes can simply attempt kicks with their non-preferred side (the left leg for a right-footed kicker and vice versa). For almost every player, the non-preferred leg can be viewed as an unskilled version of themselves, meaning that the movements are undeveloped in comparison to their dominant side. Hence, their performance will be reduced when forcing themselves into this arrangement, often because the sequence of movements on the non-kicking side are much different than when attempting kicks with the non-preferred foot. Players tend to restrict movements in the non-kicking-side arm in an attempt to 'control the kick'.

Examining the the components we've outlined so far will often reveal the errors we've discussed avoiding and remedying in this chapter. A general, unnatural tightness will prevail over the entire movement, negatively affecting the timing, force, and even accuracy of the kick. The action of the non-kicking-side arm will often be down, back, and under the line of the shoulder—and actions that occur ancillarily to that will be restricted.

In every case, those hampered movements are the same ones responsible for errors made by athletes kicking with their preferred foot, illustrating just how vital the concepts discussed here are to the overall success of a given attempt.

CONCLUSION

As with our analysis of the leg movements that occur in each kick, the specifics of the arms shouldn't be considered a 'technique' in and of themselves so much as additional detail to inform implementation of the Momentum-Alignment-Follow through practice model. Accordingly, the key points are:

- Kicking is a whole body action, so restricting one element—in this case, the upper body—will restrict other elements of the kick.
- Extending the ball well out in front of the player is crucial in order to create 'space' for the kick.
- What an athlete does with the non-kicking-side arm is vital to the success of the overall endeavor.

By applying these principles to each phase of kicks undertaken in practice, athletes and coaches can come to better understand how each element affects the others. Ultimately, it's that understanding which will facilitate a player's ability to deliver the ball to his target with greater force and accuracy.

CHAPTER SIX
THE THE HANDS

'To play it safe is not to play.'

– Robert Altman

Imagine a footballer in a game environment, surrounded by opposition players, and in need of a way to transfer the ball to a teammate's hands. The roar of the crowd as well as the noise of the other team fill his ears as he begins the familiar movements needed to deliver a field kick to another player.

The ball cradled in his hands, he raises his arms out in front of him just as he has thousands of times before. Then, something unexpected happens, and in an effort to cling to what's safe and familiar, he fails to remove his non-kicking hand from the ball at the apex of the swing. Rather than releasing it into the care of his kicking hand as he should, he holds onto it with both hands just a bit too long before the drop—and the results are less than desirable.

Whereas the athlete's body might have moved in a predictable pattern if this phase of the kick had been executed properly, the timing of the sequence is skewed by his late release. Rather than seeing his non-kicking-side arm rotate back and arc over the shoulder while the kicking-side arm lowers and drops the ball, the non-kicking arm is forced off the ball sideways instead. There's no time for the graceful rise and fall typical to such kicks, and it's replaced by a jerking back-and-forth motion that feels weak and rushed.

The result is that there isn't enough strength in the non-kicking side of the player's body to support the kick itself, either leading to a loss of power or an errant kick that skews in the wrong direction. The sequencing of the arms and legs has been broken by the athlete's late release.

It's a scene that plays out regularly, yet fans, commentators and coaches alike often fail to notice the root cause of the problem, instead attributing the athlete's 'mistake' to poor 'ball drop', not running directly at the target, or simply not having generated enough momentum before the kick.

TIMING

The majority of coaching concerning what athletes should do with their hands all but ignores the non-kicking hand's effect on timing. Often, coaches treat timing like a magical ability players are either born with or will forever lack, when in reality, it's simply a function of sequencing the various aspects of the kicking action.

As shown in Figure 11 of Chapter 5, when release of the ball occurs at the apex of the arm swing, the non-kicking-side arm can then travel up, back and over the shoulder as the kicking-side arm lowers the ball towards the kicking foot. As the athlete swings through with the kicking leg, the non-kicking arm can then come forward underneath the line of the

Fig. 11

Fig. 11 cont.

Positioning of the hands on the ball, and coordination of the arms in preparing for a kick

shoulder—and the entire movement can be completed with stability and strength. In addition to being crucial in the timing of a kick, these movements of the non-kicking arm provide a counter-balance to the force from the kicking leg and assist in creating an 'anti-rotation' movement.

Problems arise when players have been repeatedly coached to 'stay over the ball' or 'be careful with the drop'. This advice often shifts their focus in a way that encourages clinging to the ball for too long. When they do receive specific coaching in this area, it's almost always centered around the specifics of the player's grip—something that, in and of itself, may not actually need to be altered.

After all, effective kicking is routinely observed in athletes whose grip is further down or up on the ball than is considered 'ideal'. Sometimes, the ball is also held with an asymmetric grip without any ill effects on the result of the kick.

GRIP VARIATION

In general, AFL players will cradle the ball on its bottom third with their fingers on the front half of its surface, usually with their hands placed symmetrically on either side. However, there is certainly observable variation at all levels of the game. In fact, the specifics of each person's grip are as unique as the size of their arms and the stretch of their palms. The number of AFL players who deviate from the so-called norm in this manner demonstrates that success is possible even in the absence of a 'standard' grip.

Rather than discouraging these variations, coaches should allow athletes at the junior level to grip the ball in whatever manner allows them to successfully deliver it to their foot vertically. And, as we discussed in Chapter Five, the ball in question need not necessarily be an AFL football, which may be too large for developing hands. In fact, introducing an AFL ball at a very young age may not be the best idea even if it's possible physiologically. Its shape and larger size will necessitate potentially undesirable compensations in grip (and other aspects of the kicking movement) that could be carried on to when the athlete graduates to a more senior-level league.

For those already playing at a higher level but struggling with issues related to ball release (and perhaps therefore the grip), there are other techniques for improvement that coaches and players alike might employ. Many of them are interrelated to the concepts discussed in Chapter Five: they centre around becoming less concerned with minimising the distance between the drop of the ball and the player's foot while paying greater attention to whether the kicking arm is fully extended out in front of the athlete's body in preparing for ball release. By working to ensure those movements are allowed to happen in an uninhibited way, the athlete's grip will naturally come to the appropriate position rather than being coached in reverse.

From a mechanical perspective, that makes sense: the hands are an extension of the arms, meaning the way the ball is held and the manner in which it's moved will be determined by a combination of both elements, distinct though they may be. Just as holding the ball in a 'strange' manner will restrict the movements of the arms, so too will incorrect movement of the arms have a negative effect on the relative correctness of a given grip.

That's why none of these concerns should overwhelm the foundational elements of Momentum, Alignment and Follow-through, mastery of which will likely bring about proper grip in an organic fashion when combined with the other concepts discussed in this book. While that learning process is taking place, players should feel free to adjust their grip in whatever way seems likely to facilitate execution of the complete movement.

Such training will also more readily prepare them for the chaotic nature of the sport itself, which will inevitably require the use of a slightly different grip depending on the situation in which a player finds himself. When performing a set-shot goal kick, for example, an athlete has a great deal more time to properly prepare for the shot than he does when kicking in general play, where improvisation plays a more prominent role in overall success. In practice, this may manifest itself as a more rigid grip at the front of the ball during a goal kick, whereas field kicks might see a more relaxed aesthetic.

BASIC PRINCIPLES

Still, there are some basic principles that can be observed in the grip and hand positioning of athletes throughout the sport. After all, regardless of the specific style employed by a given kicker, all are attempting to accomplish essentially the same task: to use one hand to deliver the ball to the foot.

It's in this portion of the overall movement, generally referred to as the 'ball drop', that grip becomes a significant factor. Despite the terminology used to describe the action, the ball doesn't simply fall like a stone, but forms an 'arc' brought about by the forward motion of the kicker's run-up as the ball falls toward the foot. In other words, it travels slightly in front of the player with the nose pointed out, and ideally, rotates into a vertical position by the time it connects with the boot.

With that in mind, the goal of 'proper grip', and the movements broadly referred to as 'ball drop', is to maintain control over this arc and be aware of how it changes for different kicks. The likely path of the arc during a kick executed while running at speed, for example, will be more pronounced than a kick undertaken after a single step. Between those two extremes, there are countless other situations that will necessitate slight variations in the trajectory of the arc.

Certainly, that knowledge helps emphasise the importance of getting the ball well out in front of the body during the arm extension phase. It should also point to the fallacy of being overly focused on the minutia of one's grip. So long as a player is able to transfer the momentum of his run-up in such a way that the ball arcs slightly over and arrives at the foot facing up, his grip is serving its purpose regardless of what it looks like. As we've already demonstrated, its exact appearance will vary depending on whether the kick is being executed on the run or from a static start.

FEEDBACK MECHANISMS

There are multiple feedback mechanisms that can help an athlete better understand how their grip influences the outcome in each of these situations, and like most concepts in this book, an important means of learning from them is to hold the position of the hand briefly after the drop is complete. Obviously, this brief freeze can't be held as long as those practiced in the follow-through section, but even a split second of hesitation (and awareness) at this phase can help players conceptualise how the ball left the hand and the manner in which it reached the foot.

Of course, training oneself to take this moment of introspection may well require some practice in and of itself, but it's a discipline worth developing. In addition to providing the feedback we've discussed, it's also likely to improve the overall mechanics of execution in each individual scenario. Given enough study, that knowledge will help athletes make minor last-minute adjustments in the positioning and trajectory of their kicking leg and foot based on the intuitive feel of the ball leaving their hand.

The ultimate aim is for this feedback to be so clear and easy to interpret that the athlete responsible for a kick can predict where the ball will be in space at any given moment. That level of awareness leaves him free to trust the natural movement of his arms and hands to be properly coordinated in the absence of artificially coached restrictions.

TRAINING THE MOVEMENT

Once the underlying principles have been internalised, athletes can further their understanding of the concept by varying the speed and length of their run-up and observing the changes required to deliver the ball to the foot well. Players should also change up the angles of their body as compared to the target, as this is yet another factor that will ultimately influence the way they hold the ball.

DEPARTURE FROM CONVENTIONAL WISDOM

These concepts diverge from conventional wisdom in a number of ways, ranging from the degree of flexibility I've proposed regarding what constitutes 'proper grip' to the very positioning of this chapter in the book. Coaches charged with introducing new Australian Rules Football players to the art of kicking almost always begin instruction with grip and focus on it intently, whereas I made a very conscious decision to save it for a far later point in the conversation—and give it a much softer treatment.

One of the primary reasons behind that decision should be obvious by now: there really is no such thing as an 'ideal grip', but many possible correct positionings based on the circumstances in which a given kick is executed, and the makeup of each individual player. Whereas many coaches might look to change a young player's grip in the event of an errant kick, the true problem often lies elsewhere in the mechanics of the movement, and focusing too intently on the hands can obscure other opportunities for improvement.

Instead, coaches and players alike would be better served by observing and continually improving their control over the way hand movement affects the timing of a kick. By using the tools described in this chapter to do so, they can avoid far more errors than they ever could while concerning themselves with specific grips.

PART THREE
THE MIND

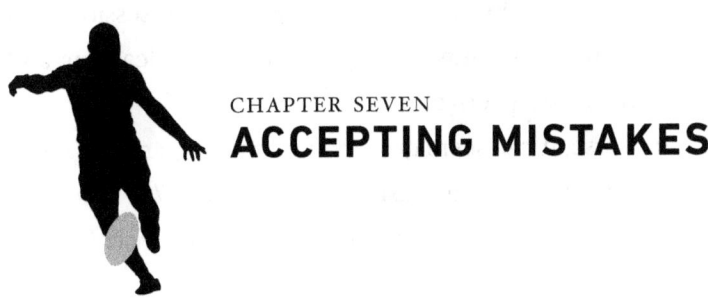

CHAPTER SEVEN
ACCEPTING MISTAKES

'Success is not final. Failure is not fatal. It is the courage to continue that counts.'

– Winston Churchill

Sometimes, things just go wrong.

A player practicing goal kicks can execute every phase of the movement correctly, make flawless contact with the ball, and still miss due to some minor error in the athlete's aim. Assuming the kick being attempted is at the more difficult end of the spectrum—45 meters away from the goal and 10-15 degrees from the boundary line, for example—the odds of this type of error obviously increase accordingly.

In and of itself, this isn't necessarily a bad thing. As we've already discussed, the very nature of Australian Rules Football leaves each kick open to a certain degree of chance regardless of how skilled the athlete participating may be. That's one of the many things that make the sport fun to watch and to play.

Where problems do often arise is in the player's response to these inevitable 'errors' in practice. When an individual is solely concerned with the outcome of each individual kick, the resulting emotional reaction to such an occurrence often sets the tone for the remainder of the practice session, and can ultimately determine its total value from a learning and development perspective.

Of course, it can seem quite natural to compare one's present results to those of the past. *That kick was terrible,* an athlete might think. *I kicked really well on Wednesday. Why aren't I kicking well today?*

Such self-scolding regarding past performance may seem like a standard part of the effort to improve, but it inevitably gives way to worries about the future. Not only is the athlete now overly concerned about the possibility of missing again, but the focus of practice has been lost and the session has simply become a test of performance.

The same could be said for a player who's overly pleased with himself after a series of successful attempts. In both cases, the focus of the session has been on performance rather than on learning.

Left unchecked, these mental gymnastics create a vicious and counterproductive cycle that ultimately does more damage to the player's well-being than a simple missed kick ever could. If the missed kick occurs in the presence of a coach who is likewise preoccupied with each effort's outcome, he'll often exacerbate the situation by offering a critique on a single aspect of the movement: 'Your ball drop went wrong', or perhaps, 'You didn't run at the target'.

In both cases, the individuals involved need to work to remove their egos from the equation and come to terms with the fact that attempting to get better at something necessarily involves making 'mistakes' along the way. That doesn't mean mistakes will happen 80 or 90 percent of the time, but they're still going to occur, and there is no single, magical answer that's going to solve the problem.

Instead of trying to analyze what went 'wrong' during each individual kick, players and coaches need to move to a judgment free mindset to fully realise the benefits of feedback from the Momentum, Alignment, and Follow-through phases of the action. Attempting to make minor adjustments to their technique from kick-to-kick does nothing to benefit the broader effort to improve across a number of practices, weeks, and months.

If a player can detach himself from the outcome of his short-term performance, however, it greatly improves the odds he'll obtain useful physical feedback from the Momentum, Alignment, and Follow-through phases of each kick. Remember, the ultimate aim of the player practicing is to be able to self-teach and self-correct, meaning he must learn a number of things simultaneously: the practice disciplines and routines needed to improve, the observational skills necessary to benefit from feedback, and the physical process of kicking itself.

Put simply, players are not only learning how to kick better—they're also learning how to practice better. The coach's role is to endow the player with a framework and environment that facilitates that kind of learning, making it vital that he encourages the athlete to observe himself in a nonjudgmental way.

Successfully applying this approach means players will neither criticise themselves nor pat themselves on the back based on the binary outcome of a single kick. It's through this type of self-assessment that athletes can avoid feelings of anger and blame in the moments after an unsuccessful kick or unnecessary self-assurance after a successful one. Instead, they'll come to value both for the skill-improving feedback they provide.

Implementing this mindset at the junior level, while still counterintuitive for players and coaches alike, should be fairly simple if it begins at an appropriately young age. After all, these players have had less time in internalise negative, unhelpful mindsets, and will probably be more open to making a change to their regimen.

Such a shift in thinking will likely be easier said than done when dealing with athletes who have been practicing under an outcome-centric model for a number of years. However, in both situations, coaches must remain disciplined in reminding players that development will take place in the span of several months, not within a single practice session—or even a week's worth of them.

It's a concept that often comes naturally to athletes competing in individual sports like golf and gymnastics, but the nature of team-based competition often encourages those involved to concern themselves principally with outcome and ongoing competition. Consider the pressure on an individual footballer, who not only has 17 teammates relying on him to kick accurately for goal and in general play, but also feels judgment from the opposing team, the spectators in the crowd, and his coaches. With so many people's opinions hinging on the outcome of each kick, it can be incredibly difficult to avoid concerning one's self with it in order to facilitate proper practice.

One way to counteract those feelings is to perform kicking practice sessions in a scaled-down environment—either alone in the case of goal-kicking exercises, or with one or two other players while training field-kicking. In fact, many AFL players learned in precisely this manner during their youths, often without realizing it. They thought they were just young footballers, kicking the ball by themselves for hours on end purely because it was a fun way to pass the time during their childhood. That they were freeing themselves of the expectations of their teammates and coaches was an unintentional benefit, but its effect on their abilities was clearly a positive one.

This isn't to suggest that practicing alone is necessarily superior to other types of practice. On the contrary, the game environment demands that AFL players make countless split-second decisions that can only be appropriately prepared for when trained under similar circumstances in practice. At any given second, an athlete's judgment will be called upon to determine whether or not to kick the ball in the first place, and if so, where they're kicking the ball, at what pace the kick should be executed, and the proper method or style for doing so.

There's a growing consensus in the world of skill acquisition which suggests that the decision-making process and the physical process are inextricably linked. Logic would therefore dictate that the most effective form of practice is one which simulates the game environment. Undoubtedly, this type of practice is a critical component of the overall training program. However, my experience with the Swans was that working on the physical elements of a kick outside the decision-making context also results in improved skill once those components are added back into the mix.

Certainly, there is a time and a place for performance-based sessions, but an athlete can't possibly offer up his best performance while still attempting to learn or improve the movement needed to produce those results. The very nature of learning means that performance will fluctuate over a period of time, hopefully trending upward as the number of sessions a player undertakes grows. Both coaches and athletes alike should aim to increase the average level of performance over an extended period of time, and that simply isn't done efficiently when every practice has the sole aim of hitting every kick 'perfectly'.

Such practices are more easily justified at the professional level, but it's simply unrealistic for junior league coaches to expect 11-12 year old players to produce ultra-consistent results. In fact, placing premium on performance at that age likely does more harm than anything, and is typically driven by the coach's ego more so than a desire to see the athletes progress.

Setting that impulse aside requires both the coach in question and his players to remain disciplined in resisting the urge to solve each individual 'mistake' in practice. By applying the principles of Momentum, Alignment, and Follow-through consistently, they can facilitate considerable improvement while maintaining focus on the correct thoughts and practice processes.

Not only will this help reduce the often tremendous amount of frustration, mental pain, and anguish involved in learning or developing a physical skill—it will ensure acquisition and mastery of the skill itself come as efficiently as possible.

CHAPTER EIGHT
FEEDBACK MECHANISMS

'You need to use your brain after the kick as much as before it. You have to retain a sense of calm. I've been guilty of it plenty of times, but if you're swearing yourself hoarse after missing a kick, it's not helping you improve. Understand why you've made a mistake and you can move forward.'

– Jonny Wilkinson

Attend any junior level practice session and you're bound to hear a great deal of binary feedback. Coaches will praise great kicks and deride poor ones in just those terms—every kick will either be a 'good kick' or a 'bad kick', and the difference between the two will be judged entirely on its outcome.

Given that we've already established the inherently harmful nature of this approach, how can coaches adjust their practices so that the feedback provided is more beneficial and contains more depth? There are a number of ways for athletes to receive feedback from the physical process of kicking, and they extend well beyond the simple nature of each effort's outcome.

From a visual perspective, feedback could center around where the ball travels in relation to the point of alignment: the angle of the ball as it leaves the foot, the distance it travels, and the arc it takes along its path. By paying close attention to these details, players can then experiment with slight alterations in the kicking action and measure their effect on the movement of the ball.

A drop punt is considered clean if the ball leaves the foot spinning backwards, end over end. For younger players, simply achieving that rotation can be an important goal pursued through these feedback mechanisms. More advanced athletes might work on adjusting the speed of the spin itself, making it faster or slower by adjusting the way it strikes the boot—itself another useful tool for acquiring proprioceptive feedback so long as it's kept stiff, providing a firm point of contact that transfers force to the ball.

Ideally, this contact should occur between the upper third of the foot and the lower third of the ball, and the impact itself should feel 'soft' against the player's body. The resulting sound can also be a source of feedback for the kicker, with properly-executed movements producing a light, soft sound as opposed to a dull thud or a sharp strike.

Once a player familiarises himself with these feedback mechanisms, he can then link them to the outcome of a given kick and begin to anticipate the ball's reaction to specific changes in the movement. Using that information, he can then apply a feed-forward approach to obtain better control over the ball by aiming to execute an individual kick so that it creates a certain feel or sound. Ultimately, each sensory signal will serve as a link to the physical processes of Momentum, Alignment, and Follow-through.

Coaches can help the athlete internalise these lessons by providing their own feedback as it applies to the Momentum, Alignment, Follow-through model—not necessarily after each kick, or even a series of kicks, but as an overall summary of a given practice session. Done in conjunction with video documentation (even if only using a phone or other mobile device), athletes can then be trained to understand feedback from an external perspective in addition to their own first-hand experiences.

That said, there's no reason video feedback must necessarily be supplemented by verbal feedback from a coach. Instead, trainers can simply package together video of particularly well-executed kicks, which will help the athlete subconsciously confirm the physical processes they've undertaken during practice.

Assuming a coach does decide to add his own commentary to the mix, the volume of that feedback should be determined on an individual basis. Athletes practicing at the sport's highest levels likely won't need as much verbal feedback as a junior player might. And in either case, the frequency with which that feedback is provided or withheld should be based on the athlete's unique temperament and skill.

If a coach notices a player generating excellent Momentum but consistently failing to maintain Alignment through their kicks, he may step in mid-session and suggest focusing on this principle through the next series of kicks. By contrast, an athlete whose errors are varied among the three distinct phases may be better served by a reserved approach that allows the self-correction process to refine itself over time. It may even be best to forgo verbal feedback entirely and let the video documentation of each session provide directions for ongoing practice.

By doing so, coaches provide players with the opportunity to strengthen the mental connection between the feeling of a successful kick and one that appears well-executed on video. In turn, this increases the degree to which they'll value being aware of the many feedback mechanisms available to them, making them more likely to pay them the attention they deserve during future practice sessions.

Certainly, erring on the side of less verbal feedback is preferable to offering too much, which can lead to the athlete becoming confused or growing dependent on a coach's words rather than using the other avenues of learning available to him. Even if that isn't the case, an overly verbal approach is still less desirable due to the potential for miscommunication. Different words and phrases carry different connotations for different people, and when there's too much conversation taking place, it can be difficult for athletes to implement the desired physical changes.

In a movement as complex as kicking, there are an almost incalculable number of issues with which a player might be confronted. If a coach is providing constant verbal feedback every time something goes 'wrong', it will be nearly impossible for the athletes in his charge to determine what he actually means and incorporate it into the movement. When things *are* going right, there's also very little benefit to be garnered by saying, 'Well done'.

It's probably obvious that this hands-off approach runs counter to the instincts of most coaches, whose natural tendency will be to provide frequent verbal instructions and feedback.

After all, they're probably quite passionate about both the sport and their charges' performance, and likely feel their value to both is in offering whatever wisdom they can provide.

An unfortunate side-effect of that attitude is that some feel compelled to provide a running commentary on how athletes are performing the technical aspects they're trying to improve. It's a trend that's especially noticeable in junior-level leagues, where the coach's feelings are regularly interjected regardless of whether they affirm what's being done or seek to correct it.

The trouble with this approach is that the verbal language used to describe corrections to the movement is different than the language of the body when undertaking a kick. First-hand feedback experienced by the kicker, meanwhile, is the direct result of the physical process. Accordingly, it's more likely to align with what the athlete feels on an instinctual level. Rather than trying to compete with that, coaches should be setting up practice scenarios that encourage it and draw attention to it.

That's best done by developing a practice structure based on the previous chapters of this book and making the footballers being coached aware of it. Then, the only commentary that's needed will be in regard to how they're carrying out the structure to which they've been introduced. In other words, the coach should reduce the number of times he says things like, 'That's poor', or, 'That's brilliant', until those phrases are almost never uttered.

Several simple activities can be used to elicit the kind of self-perceived feedback that makes such commentary unnecessary. For the first, players could be tasked with deliberately changing the shape of the ball's flight as it left the boot. In other cases, they could be directed to produce flat kicks of varying force, while in other instances they might be asked to produce kicks with a middling level of arc. Finally, a coach might ask them to execute a kick with a very high angle of flight.

Regardless of the specific type of kick used during these activities, the end goal is for each athlete to acquire and interpret feedback on how the feeling of producing the movement varied based on the end goal. They can then be instructed to deliberately change the direction the ball travels as it leaves the boot, as well as the speed with which it rotates.

Again, there are a wide variety of specific outcomes that can be used to facilitate such activities: players can be asked to spin the ball backwards as purely as possible, or cause it to spin with varying degrees of off-centeredness. But the true goal of the drill, as always, is for the athlete to become more aware of how their body feels when creating different movements (using the principles of Momentum, Alignment and Follow-through to direct feedback).

Similar drills can be run varying other elements we've already discussed, including the point of impact on the ball, the sound the impact makes, and the feel of the ball on the foot. At their conclusion, the athletes being trained should begin to anticipate the feelings that lead to each outcome prior to undertaking their kicks, with the aim of producing a better outcome during future movements.

The challenge for coaches running each of these drills is to determine whether or not they'll provide verbal feedback at all, and if so, whether they want to positively reinforce 'correct' kicks or offer direction when 'mistakes' occur. If a coach does decide to provide feedback, he'll need to have a very clear idea of what he hopes to see in a correct movement versus one that needs to be altered. Ideally, these decisions will be made within the context of the Momentum, Alignment, and Follow-through model. Then, he'll also need to determine the frequency with which he intends to offer said feedback.

With such a wide range of possibilities, the practical application of the practice session could look quite different depending on what course of action a given coach chooses to pursue. If the activity is based on the feel of contact with the boot, for example, a coach may decide to grade each kick on a scale of one to five, encouraging each athlete to create associations between the feelings of a 'good' kick and the word used to describe it. He may similarly decide to provide the exact same type of feedback only after ten kicks have been completed, or only after the conclusion of an entire practice session.

Alternatively, coaches might choose to offer instruction only after performance falls outside a certain range of acceptability. Or, they might decide to offer no feedback at all unless specifically requested by the player.

If the athletes themselves are struggling to connect the feeling of their kicks with their outcome, the coach can then add a video component to the practice on a semi-regular basis. After seeing themselves perform the action over time, they will often become more aware of the movements leading up to each kick, thus facilitating better awareness.

Another technique that, while counterintuitive, may prove beneficial is called 'amplification of error'. A coach implementing this methodology would ask the athletes under his direction to deliberately over-exaggerate the primary error in the skill being practiced. A right-footed kicker, for example, would be asked to intentionally perform a dramatic twisting movement with their left side, exercising no control over their non-kicking limbs (and therefore losing control of their alignment). Similarly, players who are struggling to get the ball out in front of their body and hunching up could be encouraged to deliberately bend forward to an excessive degree and drop the ball extremely close to their kicking foot.

The primary advantage of this mode of instruction is that it very clearly demonstrates the flaws of performing the movement incorrectly, and requires no verbal instruction that might be misinterpreted by the athlete. Instead, he can compare the outcome of different movement patterns with their end results and create a better understanding of what not to do in an organic way.

A coach's role in this methodology is to ensure that the error being amplified is one integral to the execution of the movement. In other words, they should be fundamentally critical to the Momentum, Alignment, or Follow-through phases of the kick. Anything else should be considered secondary and can probably be corrected with compensatory adjustments.

As with each of the training recommendations discussed in this chapter, the ultimate goal is for the athlete to leave the session with a greater understanding of what correct execution feels like. The more refined that connection becomes, the more likely any player is to see results.

Facilitating that connection in this manner relies on three essential practice components:

- The use of the Momentum, Alignment, Follow-through model for directing feedback;
- Understanding that feedback itself can be gathered from many sources other than the outcome of the kick;
- And varied degrees and types of verbal feedback offered by a coach.

With these elements in place, athletes will be ideally positioned to learn and better internalise the intricacies of the kicking movement.

CHAPTER NINE
GOAL KICKING

'You must be able to accept the painful truth that you might miss.'
— Anonymous

It starts with a professional footballer who's having an off night.

Perhaps he misses a set-shot early on, and before he knows it, one has turned into two, which then gives way to three. As his performance continues to suffer, it becomes clear something needs to change—and in the absence of a sound practice feedback method, the 'change' in question can be some apparently minor tweak in technique, often selected on the fly.

I'm going to reduce my run-up by four steps, he might think. *When I did that last weekend, I was more successful, so that must need to happen with every kick going forward.*

It may sound odd when it's written out like that, but from reading articles focused on players' goal kicking, it becomes obvious that players react to short-term success or failure with similar 'changes'. It's possible for athletes to spend their entire careers bouncing between success and failure as they make minor alterations to their technique depending on those outcomes.

While there is certainly a time and a place for high-level athletes to make changes to their technique, those changes should be based on a sound structure for practice, learning and feedback—and driven by observations made based on this practice method. When it's a spur of the moment decision made in response to a handful of missed shots, it's usually an indication that the player is confused or uncertain about exactly what's going wrong (or what's working correctly).

In part, this stems from an inability or unwillingness to accept the very likely possibility that they might miss. Many competitors seem to expect to hit 80 or 90 percent of their attempts while failing to realise that even the most successful players in the sport's history kick only seven of ten set shots for goal across the course of their career. As we've already established, the very nature of Australian Rules Football dictates that a certain number of shots will almost certainly be missed no matter what, illustrating the pointlessness of overreacting to the outcome of a handful of attempts.

Instead, athletes should take it as a cue to return to the fundamentally sound practice and feedback methods advocated in this book. Continue to rehearse the physical and mental disciplines that create effective improvement, and rely on those rather than the outcome of a given kick in a given game or practice session.

Set-shot goal kicking is where all of those principles come together, making it an ideal measure of the degree to which they've been internalised by the player. That said, a set-shot goal kick is unique among activities undertaken in an AFL game environment because it's the only time an athlete will be called upon to slow down and focus solely on kicking. Setting aside issues of fatigue, it can be quite difficult for an athlete to shift mental focus from running, tackling, kicking on the run, and applying a game plan to simply performing a single controlled motor skill—particularly one as complex as kicking.

The situation is further exacerbated by the expectations of the player's teammates, who are relying on him to score points after moving the ball from one end of the field to the other, and the distracting sledging of the opposing team and crowd. Each of those factors exists in addition to the complicating variables inherent to any AFL kick: the double-accuracy demands of correctly dropping the ball and propelling it through the goal; the oval shape of the ball interacting with the convex surface of the foot; and the roar of the crowd, both for and against the goal kick presently taking place.

With these added layers of complexity in play, the hours spent practicing the disciplines of Momentum, Alignment, and Follow-through become all the more critical. They are what will allow the kicker to execute each phase of the movement correctly during a game without being distracted by external issues—or the player's own mindset.

When errors occur during this aspect of a game, closer examination will reveal they're almost always the result of insufficient momentum prior to the kick, incorrect or poor alignment control through impact, or inadequate follow-through. As we've already discussed, the movement functions as a chain, meaning that all three problems are inextricably linked. A lack of physicality in the runup to a kick may give way to inadequate momentum, which can lead to issues with alignment and follow-through in turn.

There are countless factors that could cause the initial error: fatigue, lack of mental focus, and a desire to 'be careful' with the kick are all possible explanations. Regardless of those factors, the end result is the same. The kick is inaccurate or lacks the necessary power to reach its target, and an opportunity to score is missed.

Such an error cannot be attributed to a simple lack of ability, as any athlete playing at the professional level is more than capable of successfully kicking at goal from up to 50 meters, and can generally kick the ball straight. However, when practice sessions are centered around trying to control every detailed physical element of the kick—or, more destructively, too focused on the outcome of each effort—it creates uncertainty in the player's mind which goes on to manifest itself in the game environment.

DEVELOPING THE PROPER MINDSET

Consider the mental state of an athlete who only spends his practice sessions trying to hit an arbitrary number of 'successful' shots as opposed to rehearsing and developing the physical progression of each movement. Rather than using a repeatable and consistent practice method to improve the quality of each kick, he's been wholly consumed with outcome—a mindset which can produce a number of problems.

Chief among these issues is that the player may not be learning anything from the process. Remember, 'success' or 'failure' is performance—*not* learning. If players are trying to learn to kick straighter, they should be aiming to obtain feedback from each kick as to why the ball did not go where they wanted it to (or why it did go where they were aiming). Negative reactions to the outcome of each kick *ruin* the learning process, preventing players from acquiring feedback effectively. Associating only emotional feelings with goal kicking—or any kicking—practice will influence future learning and performance in a negative way.

This cannot be underestimated. Most of us grow up thinking that we should 'scold ourselves' for making errors while learning a complex skill such as kicking. However, we should in fact detach ourselves on an emotional level during practice, and aim to obtain physical feedback from each kick.

Experience matters beyond its momentary subjective impact. If a player is shouting and screaming at himself, or simply engaging in a one-off 'competition' with mates, mental images are created which are destructive to learning and performance. Physical changes occur in the brain as a result of every experience a person engages in, therefore a goal-kicking practice should be set-up in order to increase an individual's capacity to learn and perform in the future.

Another problem with practices focused solely on outcome is that they can cause the player to lose touch with the idea that every kick in a game environment is a standalone event. After all, hitting 15 out of 20 kicks in practice means little when the player misses the one that had the potential to put points on the scoreboard.

Much like a basketball player required to sink 20 consecutive free throws before he's allowed to leave practice, the athlete is training for a scenario that will never come to pass in a game environment. By contrast, there will be countless circumstances in which a player will need to sink the shot immediately in front of him.

Despite this fact, practices are often organised around the opposite premise, reducing the opportunity for learning and replacing it with something that more closely resembles a competition with one's self or one's teammates over a series of kicks. In a game environment, it all comes down to just one kick—and it's more likely to be successful if the athlete attempting it has spent his all of his practices acquiring feedback on the Momentum, Alignment, and Follow-through of each movement. Even though those phases will be examined for similarities over a block of 10-15 kicks, the player should always be working to develop the mental discipline needed to focus solely on the one kick they're about to attempt.

It may sound simple, but it's much easier said than done. Focusing on a single moment can be quite difficult, particularly when the distractions mentioned above are all working in concert to defeat your attentions. By training the discipline needed to do so in the relatively distraction-free practice environment, players can more effectively tune out anything that doesn't help them kick successfully when it matters most.

With that in mind, set-shot goal kicking practice should be centered around the following principles:

- Athletes should begin each kick from a position of physical stability—preferably not bending over or twisting the ball unnecessarily in their hands;
- Players should also finish the kick in a position of physical stability—preferably following through in the direction

they want the ball to travel, not veering off to one side or the other;
- After finishing the kick, players should review how their shoulders and hips were aligned at the point of impact;
- Footballers should not worry about or become emotionally attached to the outcome of any individual kick.

This isn't to suggest that kicking the ball through the goals consistently isn't important—it unquestionably is. But it's also overemphasised in nearly every practice session occurring at every level of the sport, usually to the detriment of improving the physical action of kicking over a period of weeks, months, or even years.

As we've already established, such a focus encourages players to react emotionally to the outcome of a single kick, which often leads to a downward spiral of negative feelings and progressively worse kicks. Alternatively, an athlete might execute the movement poorly but still manage to kick a goal, eliciting unnecessary positive emotions in the process.

In either case, the footballers in question are missing out on valuable feedback they could be receiving on the physical process itself because their internal state is too dependent on its outcome. With their focus consumed by the success or failure of the kick rather than its mechanics, they lose the mental connection to their physical actions. There's too much mental clutter for them to be able to read the feel of their runup, the nature of the ball's impact with their foot, or how it travels off the boot. In the end, all they've taken away from the practice session is how many balls went through the goals versus how many didn't.

There are a number of strategies a coach might use to prevent this dynamic from taking hold. One simple method would be to ensure each practice begins with kicks of a less challenging nature before progressing to more difficult efforts. A kick of 25 meters, for example, relieves much of the 'pressure' to succeed from the athlete performing it, allowing him to focus more attention on the mechanics of the movement itself. The coach in charge of the session should be actively encouraging this mindset by reminding players to spend the follow-through and finishing portion of the movement reviewing their physical form, stability, and alignment through to the end of the movement—and not whether the kick itself went through the goals.

The value of warming up with short kicks notwithstanding, varying the distances from which kicks are attempted is obviously important once a player is properly prepared. Certainly, lower-intensity practices can remain in the 20-35 meter range, but there should also be days when athletes are also asked to increase their distance up to 50 meters just after warming up.

The purpose for this variation is to mimic the unpredictable nature of the game environment, as well as to practice the changes in technique required by longer kicks. It's obviously impossible to anticipate the distance and angle from which a player will be called upon to kick during a game. Players must be prepared to kick from any distance at any time, something that's much easier to do if they've been conditioned to do so in practice.

KICK ROUTINE DEVELOPMENT

Another piece of conventional wisdom with questionable logic is the notion that developing a pre-planned physical routine for set-shot goal kicking is an essential starting point to a player's success. On the contrary, in many cases it can actually be quite harmful to the timing and rhythm of the kick—particularly if it's forced on an athlete rather than allowed to develop naturally over time.

Much like formulating a free throw sequence in basketball, players should be allowed to settle into their own physical process over a period of weeks, months, or even years. It's hard to imagine a coach instructing each player to dribble three times and spin the ball in their hand once before taking a shot—yet athletes are routinely observed taking these exact actions instinctually as part of their preparation. Why? Because it's a repeatable action which primes the mind and body for the rhythm of a controlled event.

In Australian Rules Football, athletes at the junior level are often pushed to emulate the set shot routines of some of the AFL's top power forwards: they're instructed to walk a number of steps slowly, jog in and then kick. While that routine may be the best physical process for the professional athlete being imitated, it may not be quite right for the player being coached to use it. Certainly, it can't be applied to a large number of players as a blanket rule, as each of the footballers being trained will vary in body type and general physiology.

Even in the AFL itself, players are often told to 'come up with a goal-kicking routine', despite the fact that those same players likely already had a number of things they were doing before, during, and after each kick. These activities were simply performed at a subconscious level before, instead of being laid out and formalised verbally.

Instead of asking the athletes in question to put conscious thought into creating the routine, they could simply be videoed over a series of shots, allowing the existing routine to become self-evident. By making the players aware of it—and perhaps tweaking certain parts of it, if necessary—these coaches could achieve the same goal without risking confusion or wasting the mental resources of the players (as well as negatively impacting the physical processes already being undertaken).

That's certainly preferable to forcing such athletes to conform to a routine that doesn't naturally occur to them, which tends to cause a number of things to go wrong.

HANDLING FATIGUE

When playing under the fatigue brought about by game-like activities, players often drift away from applying the same process they've been using in low-intensity practice. This mental failure can manifest itself in a variety of ways, ranging from the common mistakes we've already covered—lack of momentum, failure to control body rotation through impact, and failure to follow-through with the kick—to an overall lack of physicality in the kick as a whole.

The latter error can be especially noticeable in kicks attempted from a short distance. The player often attempts to be too careful, overthinking the kick and slowing down as a result. The resulting loss of momentum can lead to a loss of control in alignment and rotation, both before and after impact, which is then visible in the player's follow-through. In other words, a lack of mental commitment leads to a lack of physical commitment, which causes something in the Momentum, Alignment, Follow-through sequence to go wrong.

One way players can learn to 'switch on' their goal kicking process is to practice abdominal breathing before every set shot in training. This will help players reduce their breathing rate during a game, which will likely be high following a mark. Forcing themselves to draw relatively long, deep breaths into the abdomen rather than short, quick ones often allows athletes to trigger feelings of calm control in situations that are anything but. By contrast, short, fast breathing tends to switch on feelings of anxiety or even fear—emotions that are can already high in a fast-paced game environment.

Perhaps more importantly, making the conscious decision to breathe in this manner may reinforce a player's mental link to the physical process of the set-shot kick. By taking this action in practice situations, they can sometimes anchor the mental and physical processes to one another with the breathing acting as the 'on switch' for shifting to the appropriate mindset.

SHORT RANGE VS. LONG RANGE KICKS

It probably goes without saying that different issues in the physical process can arise when a player is forced to kick at varying distances. At the shorter end of the spectrum, it's possible for almost every footballer to run straight at the goal, swing their kicking leg relatively 'straight' and cover the distance easily.

At longer distances (from 50-55 meters out, for example)

there are a different set of a concerns. Kicks in that range require a large amount of power, and are likely occurring at the limits of the player's ability. With that in mind, it should be obvious that athletes will almost certainly need to adjust their technique if they hope to achieve the required distance while maintaining the alignment needed to kick accurately.

Being prepared for those situations is a matter of practicing kicks at that distance with a focus on controlling the additional rotation of the hips and the anti-rotation of the upper body necessary to generate sufficient force. As we've already established, it will require coaches to allow for more of an arc in the kicking leg than would typically be deemed acceptable under the principle of 'kicking straight' or 'running straight at the goal'. (see figures 4 and 5 in Chapter 2 for examples of this increased 'arc').

Unless the player undertaking the movement is exceptionally tall and strong, they'll need to use more rotation of the hips and upper torso if they are to have any hope of a successful kick. Practicing this distance-based distinction is critical, both so that players are aware they can do so in a game and because it may not necessarily come naturally to some athletes.

These practices can still be undertaken using the Momentum, Alignment, Follow-through model, but players will need to tweak the manner in which they generate momentum to compensate for the additional 'rotation' or 'arc'. As a result of those variations, the follow-through will also look a bit different due to the large arc of the kicking foot and the cross-body trajectory of that movement. Counterintuitively, players will usually move forward less after impact following a long set shot; however, control of this movement should still be practiced.

AIMING

The training we've discussed so far can be rendered meaningless if the athlete can't aim their kicks correctly, making practice of this element another crucial factor to a player's overall success. Although there's a great deal of discussion from commentators and spectators about aiming at goals, it's rare to hear a player verbalise how they go about doing so. And unlike kicks in general play, which generally seem to be directed where they need to go quite successfully, the results of goal kicking can be quite inconsistent—much to the frustration of observers, coaches and the athletes themselves.

In fact, if I had a dollar for every article that's been written about how bad set-shot goal kicking is, how much worse it's getting, or why it hasn't improved, I'd be a rich man. Spectators and media personalities alike are perpetually frustrated by the 'lack of consistent performance in this phase of the game', yet few solutions to the problem are provided other than 'they need to practice more'.

One reason for the apparent difference in results between set shots and kicks attempted in general play may be found in the nature of these activities and how their specifics affect the way a footballer approaches aiming. When a player attempts a kick to a teammate, he subconsciously takes into account a number of geometric variables: the line, the distance from himself to the target player, and the flight path necessary to connect the two. The outward trajectory of the ball is planned—even if only at a subconscious level—well before the kick is undertaken, and it is consequently more likely to reach its target.

Stand the same player in front of the goals and the number of variables considered is often reduced to one: the 'line'. The goalposts are viewed as a two-dimensional target, and little thought is given to the fact that the ball must necessarily travel through and past them in order to score. If athletes were to apply the kind of 3D conceptualisation that's used in field kicking to kicking at goals—particularly in a practice environment—that awareness could go a long way toward minimising inaccuracy in that phase of the game.

Another reason the aiming process may be skewed is that players aim as if kicking from the point at which they're standing (i.e., the start of their runup). In reality, the athlete is actually kicking from a point 5-10 meters in front of their starting position, which requires a different aiming calculation—particularly if their runup is even slightly curved.

With that in mind, it's vital that any targeting method for improving set-shot goal accuracy takes this discrepancy into account. Simply 'lining up' the goals at the beginning of the run up isn't enough—players must choose a target trajectory that reflects the actual position from which the kick will likely occur as well as the eventual target.

One way to do so would be for the kicker to pick a target behind the goals with which to aim his kick. To more closely emulate the traits of player-to-player kicking, players will need to envision a flight path for the ball and kick to replicate it. This isn't to suggest footballers should be spending a great deal of time rehearsing the image itself, but by briefly considering it, they're more likely to take into account the other geometric variables that lead to increased accuracy.

An alternative way to achieve the same result might be to determine where the ball should land, essentially recreating the same mental process used in field kicking. Athletes can select a stationary object behind the goal and kick to hit it rather than simply using it to line up the shot.

Another process many of today's kickers use to refine the accuracy of their set shot goalkicking starts with marking the point from which they want to kick, usually a few meters in front of the man on the mark. Then, they move back to the end of their run-up, and begin their set shot process from that position.

This last process could be done in tandem with one of the other strategies mentioned above to assist with a player's accuracy. What really matters is that selecting any of these strategies sets up everything else required to make it a successful kick.

The necessary momentum before impact, the proper alignment at impact, and the correct follow-through will tend to come about if the player is focused on generating the correct external trajectory for the ball to hit a pre-determined landing spot. Built on top of the processes described in previous chapters of this book, it should free the mind from being overly concerned with the detailed physical elements of kicking and replace those considerations with a simpler one: generating the correct flight path for the ball.

It may seem at times that goal kicking—set shot goalkicking in particular—is looked on as an afterthought in AFL practice sessions, a point commentators can be heard making routinely. In a way, that attitude makes sense, as there are a vast number of other things which must be done correctly in order to reach a point in a game where these skills will prove useful. But what good are these other elements if they fail to deliver points at their conclusion?

After all, that's how winning is achieved.

CONCLUSION

It should be clear by now that improving an athlete's goal kicking can't be done by simply making minor tweaks to the player's 'technique' after individual kicks. A holistic approach which focuses on both the mental and physical aspects of the action is more likely to yield positive results. Below are some key philosophies to apply when practicing goal kicks:

- Athletes and coaches must recognise that performance is not the same thing as learning—and set up practice sessions to facilitate the latter rather than the former.
- As mentioned before, Momentum-Alignment-Follow-through forms the foundation for the learning and practice process.
- The physical routine an athlete undertakes prior to the kick should be allowed to develop organically in most cases, and need not be the result of instructions from a coach.
- Deep, abdominal breathing during this process may help players cope with the fatigue that commonly results from the game environment.
- Aiming a goal kick must be done by considering all of the possible factors that might affect it, creating a complete target trajectory in their mind prior to undertaking the kick.

By practicing these principles and applying them in the competitive environment, players will be better suited to increase accuracy in the set-shot goal kicking phase of the game—and hopefully silence a few critics in the process.

CHAPTER TEN
FIELD KICKING

'It's a day-long process. I don't shoot shots just to shoot shots. I'm always working in a rhythm, working on mechanics. I've got a checklist of the things I'd need to do with my form, my legs, my arms, all of my mechanics. I never casually shoot shots, ever. I shoot the same way every time. I shoot the same shots that I'd shoot during the game.'

– Kyle Korver

If there's one tendency common to practice sessions across any number of sports, it's the temptation for coaches to expect that the session will be executed flawlessly—and the AFL is no different. Whether training is taking place at the junior grades or at the highest level of the sport, there's a strong urge for those in charge to assume every kick, handball, and mark should be executed perfectly and the ball moved efficiently from one end of the ground to the other.

A potential result of that mentality is that many practice sessions are set up for repetitive success—and because performance is often valued over learning, the coach's desire for flawless maneuvering can often leave athletes feeling like anything less than constant success amounts to failure.

Obviously, there are certain points in a season when that approach is useful and even necessary. However, as we've already established, when the goal of a training session is to improve the skills of the athletes being trained, their performance will likely fluctuate as they work to refine their abilities. By its very nature, growth means they'll be operating at the outer limits of their existing skillset, and it goes without saying that results are rarely consistent when pushing the boundaries of one's aptitude.

Ignoring this fact, coaches can be tempted to continue to push for performance, leading them to arrange practices in a way that greatly reduces the variety of kicks undertaken by the athletes being trained as compared to what they'll experience in a game environment. Generally speaking, a narrow selection of kicks are repeated rather than the rich variety demanded during competition.

As a result, the number of decisions a player must make are similarly limited: when they receive the ball, they already know to whom they're going to kick or handball, how far away that player is, and that no opponents will be standing in their way. In other words, drills are conducted with a level of certainty about key aspects of each movement that will never be replicated in a game environment.

While there's no need for every single practice to be an all-out re-creation of what players will face while competing, the sport as a whole could benefit from a better balance between the two extremes. Certainly, at the junior level, the number of controlled drills is drastically higher than the amount of practices designed to replicate the requirements of the game environment.

It's a trend that's especially troubling when it comes to developing the primary skill involved in distributing the ball among teammates: field kicking.

TWO TYPES OF PRACTICE
Although the execution of a field kick may vary based on strategic needs, the ultimate purpose is for an athlete to ensure his team maintains possession until they're within a kickable distance of goal—a crucial part of the game that warrants the large number of practice sessions typically used to focus on it.

The problem is, the sessions are often as repetitive and restrictive as those imagined in the opening to this chapter. It's not at all unusual to see players simply kicking the ball around the ground to each other without any thought given to developing the physical components of the kick itself or honing the decision-making skills needed to do so effectively in a competitive environment. All they're trying to do is hit a target (in this case, their teammate).

Much like the standard mindset in set-shot goal kicking, this type of practice encourages players to think in terms of outcome dependence: a kick is either good because it hits its target, or bad because it doesn't. While there is certainly a time and a place for such training, there should also be sessions focused on the purely technical aspects of the movement itself. And, at the other end of the spectrum, there should be sessions that replicate things likely to happen in a game—moving the ball around quickly, kicking it to a teammate who's up against an opponent, or making a split-second decision between three or four potential targets.

The technical aspects of the kick can be addressed using the methods we've already outlined in this book. Game-based training, on the other hand, requires a slightly different approach, beginning with determining exactly what scenarios need to be practiced most.

GAME-BASED TRAINING

One way of determining the game-like circumstances athletes should be training is to analyze video footage of a game and determine the scenarios in which most kicks are taking place. For example, a coach might ask himself:

- How many are occurring after the player marks the ball and pushes back, effectively making it a stationary free kick?
- How many are kicked in fewer than four steps due to pressure from the opposing team?
- How many are kicked within four to eight steps?
- How many are kicked after more steps than that?

The answers to these and other questions like them can be quite instructive for coaches and players alike when compared to the type of kicks being undertaken during a given week's training. This analysis will probably reveal that players have more time to set up kicks in practice than they do in a typical competitive environment. After all, an athlete's natural instinct is to set himself up in the best position to execute a kick. Since the practice environment frees him from the practical constraints inherent to competition, he's able to take measures that aren't typically feasible in a game scenario.

Of course, such observations should not only be limited to the player undertaking the kick. Particularly with field kicking, it's worth paying attention to what the receiver of a kick is doing prior to and after receiving the ball. Are the the majority of kicks in training made to 'lead up targets' who are running directly at the kicker so that he can take a mark on the run more easily? If so, it's unlikely that the practice session mirrors what the team will typically see in a game, when the circumstances necessary to facilitate that scenario only arise during about one fifth of the kicks undertaken.

In competition, receiving players will take any number of actions to create space for the kicker, resulting in any number of possible scenarios:

- The receiving player might run at an angle in order to evade opposition players.
- If the receiver is a key forward in the forward 50, he may be standing still due to congestion in front of him, forcing the kicking player to aim the ball to his teammate's advantage.
- There may be space behind the play, requiring the kicking player to launch the ball over everyone's heads—and count on the receiving player to run backward to maintain possession.

If one compares how many times these situations happen in a game to how much time is spent practicing for them, the degree to which the practice setup doesn't reflect common game scenarios will become clear. To fix the discrepancy, coaches should run their players through activities that simulate game-like kicking, decision-making, and player movement off the ball. Players will therefore get a better sense of the variety of kicks they'll need to execute in the game environment, and by practicing that variety, they'll improve their in-game accuracy. Even better, if the activities also simulate the pressure of an opposing team trying to throw them off, athletes can increase the speed with which they make decisions on the field and how accurate the results are. All told, practice sessions like these will translate to better kicking accuracy on the field when it really counts.

Again, these aren't necessarily changes that should be implemented in every practice, but in sessions where the goal is to challenge and ultimately extend the players' game-based abilities, they can prove quite beneficial. Just make sure they're accompanied by an overall willingness to accept mistakes.

Within the last 5-10 years, this type of practice has certainly reached a higher level of prominence among Australia's professional clubs, which have increasingly moved away from predictable, cone-based drills to more game-centric ones. At the junior level, however, there is still plenty of room for coaches to implement more game-based activities, particularly in the form of mini-games that don't necessarily require a full 18 v. 18 arrangement of players.

HOW TO SIMULATE THE GAME ENVIRONMENT

One increasingly popular model for incorporating this type of training into everyday practice is referred to as the constraints-led approach to skill acquisition. The methodology is composed of variables that fit into three classifications: individual constraints, environmental constraints, and task constraints.

In field kicking, an individual constraint might be the player's size, length of limbs or overall physical fitness. It might even be a mental skill like confidence, emotional control or general motivation. Even decision-making skills and pattern recognition could be grouped under the same category. By contrast, environmental constraints might be temperature, lighting, or the terrain on which the game is being played. Task constraints, meanwhile, typically refer to how the rules of the game apply to the action being undertaken.

Using these classifications, a coach can manipulate or restrict certain constraints in training in order to facilitate the emergence of a specific movement or behavior—whether that means determining what needs to be trained, or training a previously-identified weakness in skill.

One of the easiest ways for a coach to use this method in simulating pressures of the game environment is by placing time constraints on existing drills. For example, players might be asked to close their eyes at the beginning of an activity, and be required to take action within 2-3 seconds of opening them (i.e., respond quickly to the scene in front of them). Alternatively, a coach might require players to kick within four steps of receiving the ball, or begin drills with their backs facing the action and execute immediately upon turning around.

Likewise, the physical pressure of the game environment can be simulated without the risks inherent to unnecessary tackling. For example, a coach might decide that any time an opposition defender comes within one meter of the ball carrier, the ball is automatically turned over and the activity starts again. Similarly, coaches could limit the area in which receiving players are allowed to mark the ball, forcing them to remain within a certain zone or zones marked by cones. Athletes may even be required to mark kicks in a specific manner, whether with a single hand or with both hands but only between the bottom of their chest and the top of their head.

Varying the tempo with which practice is conducted, already a common practice in most Australian Rules Football circles, also falls within this brand of training. Additionally, coaches might institute more strict control over the specific behaviors of each side in a game-like activity. In the latter example, offensive and defensive players would be instructed to undertake certain specific actions—two defenders double-teaming a particular forward or the attacking team attempting to move the ball down the field in a specific manner, for example. Then it would be up to the individuals participating in the activity to respond appropriately to the new stimulus.

Coaches might also deliberately manipulate the auditory messages a player receives in order to challenge that athlete's decision-making process. Facilitating that type of practice is as simple as setting up a drill in which four of five possible targets are calling for the ball, but the silent fifth player is the most appropriate target. Obviously, the silent target would alternate between the athletes in each iteration of the drill, forcing the kicker to stay sharp and focused if he hopes to complete the exercise.

Augmenting training activities with any of these suggestions adds time and physical constraints that force the athlete to make quick decisions, increasing what is commonly referred to as the cognitive load—the amount of working memory required to perform a task. Depending on the skill levels of the players involved, they need not be as complex as the exercises outlined above. In many cases, something as 'simple' as asking a player to call the names of all the players in his immediate area while executing a kick could adequately increase the cognitive load.

CONCLUSION

Anyone who's watched even a single AFL game knows that certainty, fluidity of movement, and freedom to run are all limited by the number of other players on the field and the chaos of the game. Combine that with the unpredictability created by the oval-shaped ball and the generally flexible rules of the sport, and it becomes clear that athletes are going to be forced into making a lot of decisions in a game environment. That's why it's so important that practice sessions simulate these limitations, forcing players to do similar mental gymnastics.

As we've already established, the ultimate goal of all these training variables is to create a practice environment that challenges different game-based skills by deliberately adjusting the many factors in play. Certainly, most professional clubs are already doing this to a certain degree, but at the junior level, the presence of game-like activity is almost certainly inadequate.

In large part, this is due to coaches operating on the misconception that younger athletes primarily need to repeat a high volume of 'skills' before moving on to more complex training. While extremely complex exercises may not be appropriate for beginning or intermediate level players, introducing simple variables like kicking off a different number of steps or under different pressure forces the footballer to think about how he's carrying out the action—a process which can only benefit his overall abilities.

Once that's done, he'll know how to approach the specific challenges of the game environment: how to generate momentum when there's only room to take a couple of steps, how to execute a kick with his nonpreferred foot, or how to maintain alignment when kicking at odd angles, for example.

A team full of players trained from a young age to handle these challenges will be better equipped to kick with flexibility, speed, and accuracy in a competitive environment.

CONCLUSION

'The most important factor influencing learning is what a learner already knows. Ascertain this and teach him accordingly.'
— David Asusbel

Although all team sports require a certain degree of cohesion among teammates, that aspect of play in Australian rules football is uniquely demanding. Certainly, it also requires a high level of physical conditioning and skill at the individual level, but the presence of the cohesion element necessarily increases the perceived importance of having the athletes train together.

However, skill practice alone, whether conducted individually or in small groups, will add other critical elements to the overall skill development program, and shouldn't be overlooked. Much like athletes who compete in tennis, golf, rugby or cricket, playing at a high level requires a large volume of repetition to improve the complex skills involved.

While amateur footballers likely don't have as much time to practice as those playing in the AFL, even those professionals sometimes fall short in practicing enough to improve a skill like kicking (due to any number of reasons, both planned and unplanned).

I'm not suggesting that volume alone is the one and only key to success, but it should be obvious that increasing the amount of time dedicated toward practicing a specific skill will result in improvement. The key is for that individual practice to take place under a progressive approach rooted in the fundamentals outlined in this book—not for the coach involved to point out what went 'wrong' with a player's technique during a specific attempt and then move on to the next player.

Methodologies like that aren't adequate when it comes to changing deeply-ingrained movement behaviors. In order to be useful, a practice strategy must necessarily be applicable to athletes at both the highest and lowest ends of the talent spectrum. I firmly believe that the key to this type of flexible training lies in following the Momentum, Alignment, Follow-through model outlined in this book.

After all, coaches, television commentators and fans alike all agree that consistency throughout a certain set of physical movements is what constitutes a 'good kick'—one which successfully delivers the ball to its intended target. However, each kick will vary in distance, angles, level of pressure and dozens of other factors, meaning those same movements have to be undertaken with a certain level of flexibility. That means athletes must be able to adapt the movements themselves to the situation in which they find themselves.

Beyond mastering the physical movements, footballers must also be trained to make good decisions under pressure. Athletes must learn to kick the ball in a way that allows the receiving player or players to keep things progressing toward scoring a goal. They can't just kick it randomly and hope for the best—they need to make the most appropriate decision based on the specific circumstances in which they find themselves.

For these reasons, a consistent kicking program should be aimed at improving specific points in the kicking skill, with a high volume of practice for each player, and with enough flexibility and uncertainty built into the program that athletes are prepared for the game environment.

Improvement on all of these fronts is going to come slowly (and at times 'painfully') for the athletes involved, making it crucial that they commit to the program and believe in its potential. So, in addition to structuring the program itself, coaches must create buy-in on the part of the players to genuinely improve their skills rather than simply maintaining a certain level of performance. Likewise, the coaches themselves must buy in and avoid setting up practice simply to facilitate the clean execution of skills.

As Mark Guadagnoli wrote in *Practice to Learn, Play to Win*: 'No challenge equals no learning'. Players and coaches alike must understand there is a fundamental difference between learning and performance, anticipate and accept mistakes, and trust that the process will carry them to greater success. How can they be sure? By recognising that the training activities are set up to find the weak points in an individual or team's skills so that learning can occur.

Using the framework outlined in this book, players and coaches alike can identify and eliminate those weak points over a period of weeks, months, and years. Consistently applying this holistic approach will prove beneficial to the kicking skills of footballers at any level.

ABOUT THE AUTHOR

UK-born Ben Moore played and coached cricket in his youth, and continued his affinity for athletics by pursuing a degree in Sport and Exercise Science at the University of Birmingham. A move to Sydney, Australia led to his completion of a postgraduate degree in the same field before becoming Skill Acquisition Coach at the Sydney Swans Football Club. Moore was responsible for the goal-kicking program for individual players, and provided advice and direction to coaches regarding learning environments. He has since returned to the UK where he spends his time mixing family and business with amateur level triathlons, all while keeping a keen eye on the AFL. Ben can be contacted at ben@aflskills.com

www.ingramcontent.com/pod-product-compliance
Lightning Source LLC
Chambersburg PA
CBHW070158100426
42743CB00013B/2954